FLAGS OF THE WORLD

Eve Devereux

Crescent Books
New York/Avenel, New Jersey

A QUINTET BOOK

This 1992 edition published by
Crescent Books, distributed by
Outlet Book Company Inc.
a Random House Company
40 Engelhard Avenue, Avenel,
New Jersey 07001

ISBN 0-517-07316-1

8 7 6 5 4 3 2 1

This book was designed and produced by
Quintet Publishing Limited
6 Blundell Street
London N7 9BH

Project Editor: Laura Sandelson
Creative Director: Richard Dewing
Designers: Nicky Chapman, Jill Demetriou
Editor: Lydia Darbyshire

Typeset in Great Britain by
Central Southern Typesetters, Eastbourne
Manufactured in Hong Kong by
Regent Publishing Services Limited
Printed in Hong Kong by
Leefung-Asco Printers Limited

DEDICATION

*For Alison Berry and Caroline Thomas of Red
Fox – not "too difficult", I hope.*

ACKNOWLEDGEMENTS

The Mansell Collection: p20. Williams-Hunt
Collection, School of Oriental and African Studies,
University of London: p23. Hulton-Deutsch Collection:
pp34, 42, 44, 49, 68. J. Allan Cash Ltd.: pp38, 45.
British-Israel Public Affairs Committee: p46.
Mexicolore: p58. American Flag House and
Betsy Ross Memorial: p89.

CONTENTS

INTRODUCTION

We've a war, an' a debt, an' a flag; an' ef this
Ain't to be inderpendunt, why, wut on airth is?

The US poet, essayist and diplomat James Russell Lowell (1819–91) was, of course, writing ironically in *The Biglow Papers*, his epic denouncing the pro-slavery party and the conduct of the government, but he touched a truth when he made his Yankee narrator include a flag among his list of essential possessions for the would-be independent nation. Since earliest times flags have been something more than functional objects, standards used for identification on the battlefield or to denote different allegiances. They early became symbols of human aspirations, loyalties, ideals, desires . . . and their modern-day national versions can still have a powerful effect even on those who would regard the sentiment of patriotism as nothing more than an expression of tunnel-vision and parochialism: it is not for nothing that in many countries there are strict penalties for the offence of defiling the flag, for in so doing the offender is also defiling the nation itself.

Every modern national, state and provincial flag has a story attached to it. Its colours may be of heraldic origin or, especially in the instances of many nations that established themselves within this past century, they may symbolize the ideals underpinning the setting up of the new nation – ideals that, sadly, are more often than not acknowledged in their violation, the flags of the most vicious and bloody tyrannies normally being replete with colours signifying purity, democracy, peace and goodwill. The emblems, too, generally have a significance beyond the historical, although some can be traced back for a millennium or more. In this book I have done my best to explain the symbolism of well over two hundred flags and, where relevant, to tell the often fascinating stories that lie behind their modern appearance.

Since this is a book for the lay reader, terminology that might not be immediately comprehensible to such a reader has been shunned. My apologies to heraldic purists.

The few months prior to this book's going to press have been turbulent in terms of the world's political geography. Most notably, Croatia and Slovenia have seceded from Yugoslavia and, of course, many of what were hitherto republics of the USSR have become unitary states; indeed, even as I write these words the future of Bosnia-Herzegovina – to become a unitary state or to remain a part of an already depleted Yugoslavia – hangs in the balance. All of the "new" countries recognized by the rest of the world community by the end of February 1992 are covered in this book. In some instances their establishment is so recent, however, that various basic details (e.g., their future currencies) are as yet unclear. Such information has therefore been quietly omitted.

An armed Pathan watches over the North-West Frontier which lies between Pakistan and Afghanistan, the scene of many battles.

AFGHANISTAN

Democratic Republic of
De Afghanistan Democrateek Jamhuriat

Population: 15,513,000
Capital: Kabul
Population: 913,000
Area: 252,000 sq mi (652,000 km^2)
Currency: 100 puls = 1 afgháni
Languages: Pushtu, Dari (Persian)
Religion: Islam
Economy: agriculture, food processing, textiles, leather products, natural gas, fruit, nuts

The flag of this turbulent country has changed frequently during this century, primarily in terms of the detail of the emblem; common features have been the wheatears and rising sun (since 1928), a central pulpit and niche from a mosque (earlier an entire mosque was represented), and scrollwork (sometimes with writing, sometimes without). In general, though, the overall pattern of three horizontal stripes — black, red, green — has been retained. The black is said to represent the country's dark past, the red the blood of the martyrs to freedom and the green both the country's agriculture and, as always, Islam.

ALBANIA

Socialist People's Republic of
Republika Popullore Socialiste e Shqipërisë

Population: 3,150,000
Capital: Tirana (Tiranë)
Population: 206,000
Area: 11,100 sq mi (28,750 km^2)
Currency: 100 qindarkas = 1 lek
Language: Albanian
Religion: Islam minority; atheism official
Economy: agriculture, natural gas, petroleum, chrome, copper, mining, tobacco

The name "Shqipëria" (the Albanians' name for their country) means "land of the eagle"; the double-headed eagle features in the state coat of arms, having been adopted from the Byzantine emblem by Iskander Bey Skanderbeg (1403–68; known also as George Castriota), an Albanian patriot who drove the Turks from his native land around 1443 and kept them out until his death, whereupon his compatriots caved in and the country came once more under Turkish domination. The red background symbolizes the blood shed during this and other struggles for independence; the yellow outline star was added in 1946 when the country became a communist republic, but removed from the flag in 1992.

LOCATION MAPS

The maps that are to be found with each country will, in most cases, give a clear indication of both a country's shape and location. In some instances, however, especially with islands, a clearer idea of location will be gained by consulting the continent maps on pages 107 to 112.

A

ALGERIA

Democratic and Popular Republic of
*al Jumhuriya al Jazairiya ad-
Dimuqratiya ash-Shabiya/République
Algerienne Démocratique et Populaire*

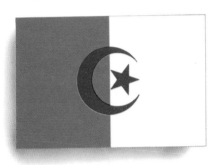

Population: 23,850,000
Capital: Algiers (Alger, El Djazair)
Population: 1,720,000
Area: 920,000 sq mi (2,380,000 km²)
Currency: 100 centimes = 1 dinar
(Algerian)
Languages: Arabic; some French; some
Berber
Religions: Islam; Christian minority
Economy: oil, gas, agriculture, fruit,
vegetables, minerals, wine, machinery

The present national flag of Algeria has been official since 1962; probably designed about 1928, it was from 1954 the flag of the independence fighters (the *Front de Libération Nationale*) and from 1958 that of the interim government. The background stripes are green, symbolizing Islam, and white, purity; these colours were also associated with Abd-el-Kader (1807–83), who, from 1832 until his surrender in 1847, led a bitter war of resistance against the French occupiers. Red commonly symbolizes bloodshed. The star and crescent are Islamic; the horns of the crescent are markedly longer than in most versions since, according to Algerian tradition, this lengthening implies good luck.

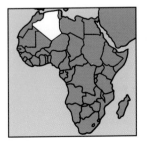

ANDORRA

Coprincipality of
*Principat d'Andorra/Principauté
d'Andorre*

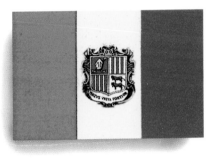

Population: 51,000
Capital: Andorra la Vella
Population: 16,000
Area: 180 sq mi (465 km²)
Currency: Spanish peseta and French franc
both in use
Languages: Catalan official language;
French and Spanish widely used
Religion: Roman Catholic
Economy: agriculture, tobacco, tourism,
postage stamps

Various possible explanations have been put forward for the colours of the three vertical stripes of the Andorran flag, but the most plausible would seem to be that they reflect the principality's joint Franco-Spanish suzerainty, blue and red reflecting the French flag and yellow and red reflecting the Spanish. Usually, but not always, the Andorran coat of arms, surmounted by a coronet, appears superimposed on the central yellow stripe.

ANGOLA

People's Republic of
República Popular de Angola

Population: 9,500,000
Capital: Luanda (Loanda)
Population: 700,000
Area: 482,500 sq mi (1,250,000 km²)
Currency: 100 lwei = 1 kwanza
Languages: Portuguese official language,
Bantu
Religions: Christianity (mainly RC),
Animism
Economy: agriculture, oil, diamonds, fruit,
coffee, mining, fishing

The yellow motif in the centre of the flag is that of the Marxist MPLA (Popular Movement for the Liberation of Angola); comprising a machete, five-pointed star and the arc of a cogwheel, it is clearly inspired by the hammer and sickle used by the USSR (now Commonwealth of Independent States). Its yellowness is said to indicate the country's natural wealth. The juxtaposed red and black of the stripes are used in other communist-liberated nations to mean "Freedom or Death"; another explanation, peculiar to Angola, is that the black symbolizes Africa and the red the spilled blood of the freedom fighters.

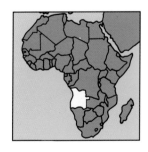

ANGUILLA
See United Kingdom

ANTARCTICA

Population: small, fluctuating and transitory
Area: 5,445,000 sq mi (14,108,000 km²)

ANTARCTIC TERRITORIES

Australian Antarctic Territory

Macquarie Islands and Heard and Macdonald Islands

Area: 2,500,000 sq mi (6,400,000 km²)

The flag of Australia (*q.v.*) is used.

British Antarctic Territory

Area: 150,000 sq mi (388,500 km²)

Until 1962 part of the United Kingdom (*q.v.*) dependency of the Falkland Islands, this territory flies the Blue Ensign with the shield from the former arms of the Falklands.

French Southern & Antarctic Territory

Area: 152,600 sq mi (395,500 km²)

The tricolour of France (*q.v.*) is flown.

New Zealand Territory

Ross Dependency

Area: 160,000 sq mi (414,500 km²)

The New Zealand (*q.v.*) flag is flown.

Norwegian Dependency

(Queen Maud Land)
Bouvet Island and Peter I Island

Area: 120 sq mi (310 km²)

The flag of Norway (*q.v.*) is flown.

South African Territory

Prince Edward Island & Marion Island

Area: 100 sq mi (255 km²)

The flag of the Union of South Africa (*q.v.*) is flown.

ANTIGUA AND BARBUDA

Population: 82,500
Capital: St John's
Population: 18,000
Area: 170 sq mi (440 km²)
Currency: 100 cents = 1 dollar (East Caribbean)
Language: English
Religion: Christianity (mainly Anglican)
Economy: tourism, cotton, sugar, rum, fruit and vegetables, fishing

Introduced in 1967, when Antigua and Barbuda became an associated state (i.e., a self-governing dependency of the UK having the right to opt for independence) and unchanged on the gaining of independence in 1981, this flag is elaborately coded. The principal colour, red, represents the dynamism of the state's people. The inverted isosceles triangle forms a victory V, the victory being, of course, that over colonialism. Reading upwards, we have white sand, blue sea and the yellow-gold of the dawning sun of the new era. The blackness of the "sky" reflects the African heritage of the majority of the islands' people.

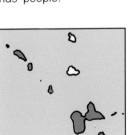

ARGENTINA

Argentine Republic
República Argentina

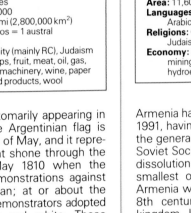

Population: 32,000,000
Capital: Buenos Aires
Population: 2,910,000
Area: 1,080,000 sq mi (2,800,000 km²)
Currency: 1000 pesos = 1 austral
Language: Spanish
Religions: Christianity (mainly RC), Judaism
Economy: grain crops, fruit, meat, oil, gas, coal, minerals, machinery, wine, paper and other wood products, wool

The emblem customarily appearing in the centre of the Argentinian flag is known as the Sun of May, and it represents the sun that shone through the clouds on 25 May 1810 when the people's first demonstrations against Spanish rule began; at or about the same time, the demonstrators adopted the colours blue and white. These colours were first formed into a triband flag in 1812 by General Manuel Belgrano (1770–1820), who for a couple of years was the leading light of the revolution, being succeeded in 1814 by José de San Martín (1778–1850). It was in 1818 that the Sun of May came to be superimposed on the white central stripe.

ARMENIA

Aikakan

Population: 3,283,000
Capital: Yerevan
Population: 1,114,000
Area: 11,600 sq mi (29,800 km²)
Languages: Armenian, Russian, Turkish, Arabic
Religions: Christianity (Armenian Church), Judaism
Economy: cotton, fruit, rice, tobacco, mining, copper, zinc, lead, hydroelectricity

Armenia has been a unitary state since 1991, having become so at the time of the general dissolution of the Union of Soviet Socialist Republics; before that dissolution Armenia had been the smallest of all the Soviet republics. Armenia was established in about the 8th century BC as an independent kingdom. In 328BC it was conquered by Alexander the Great and in 66BC by Rome; in AD303 it became the first country to adopt Christianity as its state religion, and the Armenian Church is still a distinct sect of Orthodox Christianity. Since the 4th century it has been successively under Byzantine, Persian, Arab, Seljuk, Mongol, Ottoman Turkish and Soviet rule.

A

ARUBA
See Netherlands

AUSTRALIA
Commonwealth of

Population: 16,500,000
Capital: Canberra
Population: 256,000
Area: 2,970,000 sq mi (7,700,000 km²)
Currency: 100 cents = 1 dollar (Australian)
Languages: English, Aboriginal
Religions: Christianity, Aboriginal
Economy: agriculture, meat, precious and industrial metals, oil, petroleum, wood, food-processing, machinery, manufacturing

The five smaller stars in the Australian flag (created 1901 as the winning entry in a public competition; finally given royal assent 1954), which is based on the UK's Blue Ensign, represent the constellation of the Southern Cross; this emblem has been used to token the continent since its very earliest days. Four of the constellation's stars have seven points; the fifth, which is dimmer in the night sky, has only five. The isolated seven-pointed star represents the Federal Commonwealth; until 1909 it had only six points, one for each of the states, but then the seventh was added to indicate the territories.

Australia has also the flag of the Australian Aborigines, devised in 1972. It shows a yellow disc (the sun) superimposed on two horizontal bands: the upper is black, for the Aborigines themselves, and the lower is red, both for Aboriginal blood spilled defending their country and for the land itself.

AUSTRALIA-STATES

New South Wales

Population: 5,400,000
Capital city: Sydney
Population: 3,333,000
Area: 309,430 sq mi (801,430 km²)

The emblem shows a Cross of St George, a golden lion and four eight-pointed golden stars.

Queensland

Population: 2,500,000
Capital city: Brisbane
Population: 1,138,000
Area: 591,200 sq mi (1,272,200 km²)

The emblem shows a Maltese Cross with, in the centre, a royal crown.

South Australia

Population: 1,350,000
Capital city: Adelaide
Population: 970,000
Area: 380,100 sq mi (984,400 km²)

The bird in the emblem is a Murray magpie or a white-backed piping shrike.

Tasmania

Population: 435,000
Capital city: Hobart
Population: 174,000
Area: 26,380 sq mi (68,330 km²)

Tasmania has had a red lion as its emblem since before 1855, when it was called Van Diemen's Land.

Victoria

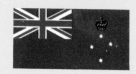

Population: 4,070,000
Capital city: Melbourne
Population: 2,865,000
Area: 88,875 sq mi (227,600 km²)

Originally without the crown and therefore very similar to the national flag, this dates back to about 1865, when it was flown by a ship of the British Royal Navy. The symbol was that of the Anti-Transportation League. The crown was added in 1877.

Western Australia

Population: 1,300,000
Capital city: Perth
Population: 969,000
Area: 975,100 sq mi (2,525,500 km²)

Until 1953, when the image was flipped, the famous black swan (badge of the Swan River Colony) faced in the opposite direction – i.e., outwards.

AUSTRALIA-ASSOCIATED LANDS

Australian Capital Territory

Population: 290,000
Capital city: Canberra
Population: 256,000
Area: 940 sq mi (2,430 km²)

The Australian national flag is flown.

Christmas Island

Population: 3,200
Centre of government: Flying Fish Cove
Population: 700
Area: 53 sq mi (135 km²)
Economy: phosphates, fishing

The flag, which is unofficial, shows a frigate bird, a simplified map of the island and the Southern Cross.

Cocos Islands

Keeling Islands

Population: 560
Centre of government: Home Island
Area: 5.5 sq mi (14.2 km²)
Economy: coconuts

The Australian national flag is flown.

Coral Sea Islands Territory

Population: 5 (approx.)
Area: 400,000 sq mi (1,036,000 km²) of which only 67 sq mi (175 km²) are land.

The Australian national flag is flown.

Norfolk Island

Population: 2,400
Administrative centre: Kingston
Population: 2,000
Area: 14 sq mi (36 km²)
Economy: tourism, fruit, vegetables

This flag was adopted in 1980. Two vertical stripes of green are to either side of a central white stripe, on which is superimposed, in the same green as the outer stripes, the stylized image of a Norfolk Island pine.

Northern Territory

Population: 136,800
Capital city: Darwin
Population: 55,000
Area: 519,770 sq mi (1,346,200 km²)

This flag dates only from 1978, when it was created by a pair of professional graphic designers, Robert Ingpen and Elizabeth Letham. The Southern Cross on the black background reflects the national flag. The stylized flower on its brownish background represents a desert rose; its seven petals indicate the desire that soon Australia will have seven, rather than six, states.

AUSTRIA

Republic of
Republik Österreich

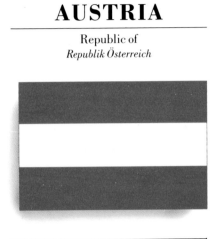

Population: 7,600,000
Capital: Vienna (Wien)
Population: 1,500,000
Area: 32,360 sq mi (83,850 km²)
Currency: 100 groschen = 1 schilling
Language: German
Religion: Christianity (mainly RC)
Economy: agriculture, fruit, meat, oil, gas, minerals, wood products, machinery, beer, wine, chemicals, textiles

Legend has it that the red–white–red stripes of the Austrian flag, certainly one of the world's oldest, had their origin during the Third Crusade of 1189–92 when Duke Leopold V of Austria (1157–94), later to be the captor of Richard the Lionheart, fought so bloodily at the Battle of Acre (1191) that the only part of his costume to remain white was a band round his middle where his belt had been. The colours have been in use since at least 1230; they took their current form as the national flag in 1918, with the dissolution of the Austro-Hungarian Empire.

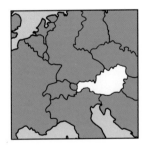

A

AZERBAIJAN

Azerbaidzhan/Azerbaydzhan

BAHAMAS

Commonwealth of the

BAHRAIN

State of
Dowlat al-Bahrain

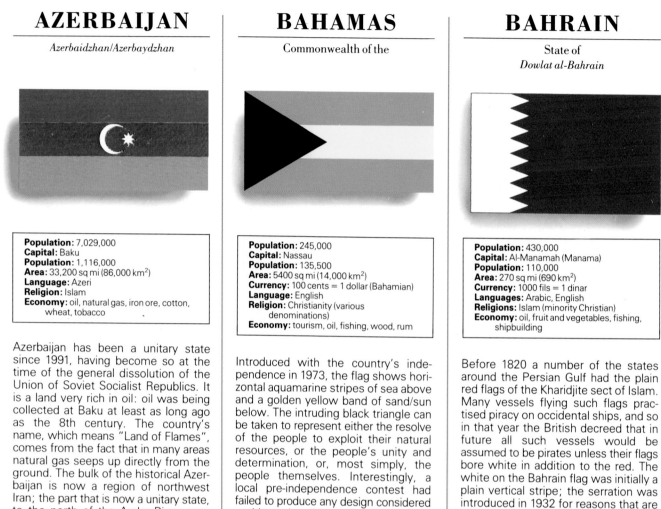

Population: 7,029,000
Capital: Baku
Population: 1,116,000
Area: 33,200 sq mi (86,000 km²)
Language: Azeri
Religion: Islam
Economy: oil, natural gas, iron ore, cotton, wheat, tobacco

Population: 245,000
Capital: Nassau
Population: 135,500
Area: 5400 sq mi (14,000 km²)
Currency: 100 cents = 1 dollar (Bahamian)
Language: English
Religion: Christianity (various denominations)
Economy: tourism, oil, fishing, wood, rum

Population: 430,000
Capital: Al-Manamah (Manama)
Population: 110,000
Area: 270 sq mi (690 km²)
Currency: 1000 fils = 1 dinar
Languages: Arabic, English
Religions: Islam (minority Christian)
Economy: oil, fruit and vegetables, fishing, shipbuilding

Azerbaijan has been a unitary state since 1991, having become so at the time of the general dissolution of the Union of Soviet Socialist Republics. It is a land very rich in oil: oil was being collected at Baku at least as long ago as the 8th century. The country's name, which means "Land of Flames", comes from the fact that in many areas natural gas seeps up directly from the ground. The bulk of the historical Azerbaijan is now a region of northwest Iran; the part that is now a unitary state, to the north of the Araks River, was annexed by the Russian Tsar Alexander I in 1813. Within Azerbaijan is the autonomous republic Nakhichevan, with a population of 295,000 and whose capital is Nakhichevan. Also still within Azerbaijan at the time of writing is Nagorny-Karabakh (population 33,000, capital Stepanakert), which seeks to become a part of Armenia (*q.v.*).

Introduced with the country's independence in 1973, the flag shows horizontal aquamarine stripes of sea above and a golden yellow band of sand/sun below. The intruding black triangle can be taken to represent either the resolve of the people to exploit their natural resources, or the people's unity and determination, or, most simply, the people themselves. Interestingly, a local pre-independence contest had failed to produce any design considered usable, and so this version was created using some of the ideas thrown up during the competition.

Before 1820 a number of the states around the Persian Gulf had the plain red flags of the Kharidjite sect of Islam. Many vessels flying such flags practised piracy on occidental ships, and so in that year the British decreed that in future all such vessels would be assumed to be pirates unless their flags bore white in addition to the red. The white on the Bahrain flag was initially a plain vertical stripe; the serration was introduced in 1932 for reasons that are unclear. It is also not clear why the Gulf pirates didn't simply add white to their flags and carry on plying their trade as before . . .

AZORES
See Portugal

BANGLADESH

People's Republic of

Population: 105,000,000
Capital: Dacca (Dhaka)
Population: 3,460,000
Area: 56,000 sq mi (144,000 km^2)
Currency: 100 paise = 1 taka
Language: Bengali
Religions: Islam (majority), Hinduism, Buddhism, Christianity
Economy: jute, tea, leather, rice, fishing, tobacco

The basic design of this flag was introduced in 1971 when Bangladesh, until then East Pakistan, succeeded after a civil war in seceding from the rest of Pakistan. The 1971 version had, on the red disc, an outline map of the country in yellow; this was dropped in 1972. The disc itself, which is not quite centrally placed (it is slightly to the left of centre), is the sun of freedom and is red for the blood spilt in attaining that freedom. The green of the background has several explanations: it is an Islamic colour; it represents fertility; it symbolizes the youth of the country; it reflects the country's lushness.

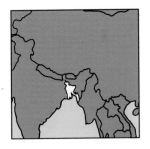

The emblem of Bangladesh

BARBADOS

State of

Population: 255,000
Capital: Bridgetown
Population: 100,000
Area: 165 sq mi (430 km^2)
Currency: 100 cents = 1 dollar (Barbadian)
Language: English
Religion: Christianity (mainly Protestant)
Economy: tourism, sugar, molasses, rum, agriculture, electrical engineering

The central vertical stripe of golden yellow represents the sands of the country's beaches. The trident of Neptune, relating to the people's dependence on the bounty of the sea, dates back to colonial times, when it was used emblematically with a shaft; when the flag was introduced on independence (1966) the shaft was removed as a sign of the break with her past. The two blue stripes are for sea and sky.

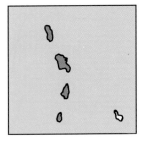

BELAU

Republic of Palau
Pelew

Population: 14,000
Capital: Koror
Population: 8000
Area: 190 sq mi (487 km^2)
Currency: 100 cents = 1 dollar (US)
Languages: English, local languages
Religion: Christianity
Economy: fishing, coconuts, cassavas, tourism

Adopted in 1981 when the islands became internally self-governing (they had earlier been under US administration as part of the UN Trust Territory of the Pacific Islands; in 1986 they signed a compact of "free association" with the USA), the flag has an off-centre yellow disc symbolizing not the sun but the moon, which represents national unity. The blue background likewise has an unexpected meaning: it is neither sea nor sky but a token of the final exit from the state of foreign administration.

B

BELGIUM

Kingdom of
Royaume de Belgique

Population: 10,000,000
Capital: Brussels (Bruxelles)
Population: 1,000,000
Area: 11,800 sq mi (30,500 km²)
Currency: 100 centimes = 1 franc (Belgian)
Languages: Flemish, French, German
Religion: Christianity (mainly RC)
Economy: engineering, automobiles, petroleum refining, mining, diamond cutting, cereals, coal

The Belgian flag is unusual in that it is almost square: the height and width are in the ratio 13:15. The black, yellow and red colours can be traced back to the arms of the provinces of Brabant, Flanders and Hainault. Arranged horizontally, they were used by the freedom fighters who succeeded in driving out the Austrians in 1789. Shortly afterwards, in 1792, the country was annexed by France, and in 1815 it was joined on to the Netherlands. In 1830 came independence and the vertical arrangement of the stripes, probably as an echo of the arrangement in the French tricolour. The shape and the arrangement were ratified in 1831.

Brabant

Limburg

Hainaut

Namur

West Flanders

Antwerp

Liège

Luxembourg

East Flanders

Armorial banners of the provinces of Belgium

Emblem of the Flemish and Walloon communities

BELIZE

Colony of

Population: 176,000
Capital: Belmopan
Population: 3000
Area: 8,900 sq mi (23,000 km²)
Currency: 100 cents = 1 dollar (Belizan)
Languages: English, Creole, Spanish, Mayan
Religion: Christianity
Economy: sugar, cereals, rum, fruit, fishing, coconuts

This flag, adopted on independence in 1981, had as its precursor the flag of the People's United Party, which led the struggle for independence from 1950, a date reflected by the fifty laurel leaves surrounding the central arms. The thin red stripes at top and bottom of the flag were added to signify the minority opposition party, the United Democratic Party. The scroll beneath the shield bears the legend *Sub Umbra Floreo* ("I flourish in the shadows"). The two men supporting the shield are, on the right, a Creole bearing a paddle and, on the left, a Mestizo bearing an axe. Behind them is a mahogany tree to stress the quondam importance of timber, especially mahogany, in the state's economy, an element yet further underlined in the three designs on the shield: top left, a paddle and hammer; top right, a saw and felling axe; bottom, a sailing ship resembling those on which the timber was ferried to Europe.

B

BELORUSSIA

White Russia
Belaruskaya

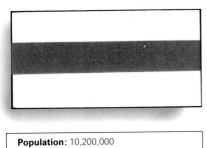

Population: 10,200,000
Capital: Minsk
Population: 1,442,000
Area: 81,150 sq mi (207,600 km²)
Languages: Polish, Russian
Religion: Christianity
Economy: oil refining, peat, engineering, cereals, potatoes, livestock, oilseed, rock salt, phosphorite, flax, hemp, sugarbeet, agricultural machinery, textiles

Belorussia has been a unitary state since 1991, having become so at the time of the general dissolution of the Union of Soviet Socialist Republics. By 1795 Belorussia had become a part of the Russian Empire, and the eastern region of today's Belorussia was made a part of the USSR in 1921, at which time the western region became a part of Poland; in 1945 this western region was annexed by the USSR. The Berezina, Dnieper, Western Dvina and Pripet rivers form an extensive network of waterways. Before the dissolution of the USSR, Belorussia was one of only two of the Soviet republics to have a separate vote at the UN.

BENIN

People's Republic of
République populaire du Benin

Population: 4,450,000
Capital: Porto Novo
Population: 132,000
Area: 44,000 sq mi (112,500 km²)
Currency: 100 centimes = 1 franc (CFA)
Languages: French, a spectrum of African languages including Yoruba, Adja, Bariba and Fon
Religions: Animism, Christianity, Islam
Economy: agriculture, palm oil, cotton, coffee, peanuts

The design of the Benin flag was adopted in 1975, three years after Lt-Col Mathieu Kerékou (1933–) had swept to power in the last of a long succession of military coups since Dahomey (as it then was) had gained independence within the French community in 1960. He established Marxism-Leninism as the system of government in 1974, and in 1975 the country's new name and new flag appeared. The overall green reflects the fact that the nation is predominantly agricultural; the red star stands for revolution, national unity and socialism.

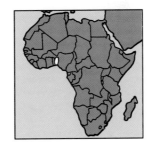

BERMUDA
See United Kingdom

BHUTAN

Kingdom of
Druk-yul

Population: 1,450,000
Capital: Thimphu (Thimbu)
Population: 20,000
Area: 18,000 sq mi (46,600 km²)
Currency: tikehung (silver money), ngultrum (paper money), rupee (Indian)
Languages: Nepali, English, Dzongkha
Religions: Buddhism, Hinduism, Islam
Economy: agriculture, rice, postage stamps, coal, limestone, wood

The wingless dragon of the flag is Bhutan's national symbol; the literal meaning of the kingdom's Tibetan name, Druk-yul, is "Land of the Dragon". Although the colours of the two triangles have varied, the current saffron yellow is an expression of the king's authority and the orange-red the spiritual power of Buddhism, the country's predominant religion.

BOLIVIA

Republic of
República de Bolivia

Population: 7,000,000
Capital: La Paz
Population: 882,000
Area: 425,000 sq mi (1,100,000 km^2)
Currency: 100 centavos = 1 peso
Languages: Spanish, Quechua, Aymara
Religion: Christianity (mainly RC)
Economy: metals, oil, gas, coffee

Bolivia was called Upper Peru until 1825, when it gained independence from the Spaniards, and Simón Bolívar (1783–1830), for whom the country was given its new name, became first president of the free nation; very soon afterwards the Bolivians realized that the exchange had not been altogether advantageous, and Bolívar in turn was driven out. The 1825 colours were, from the top, red, green and red, the green dominating the area; the following year the upper red stripe became yellow, and in 1851 the stripes became of equal area and adopted the current red, yellow, green arrangement. The red signifies the courage of the liberating army, the yellow the country's resources of metals, and the green the country's agricultural richness.

ABOVE **An engraving of Simon Bolivar, who played a major role in the liberation of Brazil and other South American countries. He became Brazil's first president in 1825 and after whom the country was named.**

The arms of Bolivia

B

BOTSWANA

Republic of

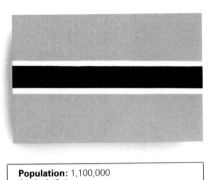

Population: 1,100,000
Capital: Gaborone
Population: 72,200
Area: 231,700 sq mi (600,300 km²)
Currency: 100 thebe = 1 pula
Languages: English, Setswana
Religions: indigenous religions (Christian minority)
Economy: diamonds, cattle, tourism, metals

Botswana's flag was adopted on independence in 1966, and the central band of black with white on either side indicates the racial harmony to which the new nation aspired; its first president, Sir Seretse Khama (1921–80), had married an Englishwoman, so the aspiration was not just an empty ideal, despite the far from harmonious relations between the races in surrounding nations, notably South Africa, on which the country's economy is heavily reliant. The overall blue expresses the concepts of sky and water, fused to represent rain: Botswana is a very arid country, and consequently the life-giving rain is of vital importance to its people – even the national motto, "Let there be rain", stresses this.

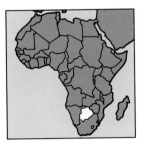

BRAZIL

Federal Republic of
República Federativa do Brazil

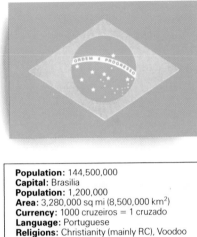

Population: 144,500,000
Capital: Brasilia
Population: 1,200,000
Area: 3,280,000 sq mi (8,500,000 km²)
Currency: 1000 cruzeiros = 1 cruzado
Language: Portuguese
Religions: Christianity (mainly RC), Voodoo
Economy: agriculture, coffee, cocoa, metals, machinery, automobiles, minerals, oil, gas, tobacco, cotton, fruit, sugar, rubber, wood products

For a long time the Portuguese owned Brazil, and it was to this nation that their royal family fled when Napoleon invaded Portugal in 1807. When they went home in 1821 they left behind them King John VI's second son, Pedro, as prince-regent. A year later he declared Brazil's independence and was crowned its first emperor. Some years later, in 1831, he was forced to abdicate in favour of his five-year-old son, who became Pedro II. Pedro I's first flag for Brazil was of green with a yellow lozenge, as in the modern version, but with the royal arms in the centre of the lozenge. The current design in the lozenge was adopted when the country became a Republic. The view is of the night sky over Rio de Janeiro on the night of the declaration of the Republic of Brazil, 15 November 1889. In the circumstances, it is a somewhat bizarre expression of liberation. The motto, *Ordem e Progresso*, means "Order and Progress".

BRUNEI

Sultanate of

Population: 241,500
Capital: Bandar Seri Begawan
Population: 50,000
Area: 2230 sq mi (5770 km²)
Currency: 100 sens = 1 dollar (Brunei)
Languages: Malay, Chinese, English
Religions: Islam, Buddhism, Christianity
Economy: oil, gas, rice, cassava, bananas

The flag of the Sultan of Brunei was originally a plain yellow. The country came under British protection in 1888, and in 1906 the diagonal black-and-white stripe was superimposed to denote that the sultan did not have absolute power, but shared it with two viziers. The coat of arms of Brunei was added in 1959, when Brunei became self-governing. It is a complex design showing a winged pillar surmounted by a pair of wings that are themselves surmounted by a flagged umbrella; the pillar is framed by a crescent bearing the state motto, "Always serve with the guidance of God"; beneath the crescent is a scroll bearing the legend "Brunei – home of peace", and to either side of it are half-spread hands to indicate the goodwill of the government.

BULGARIA

People's Republic of
Narodna Republika Bălgarija

> **Population:** 9,000,000
> **Capital:** Sofia
> **Population:** 1,100,000
> **Area:** 42,800 sq mi (111,000 km²)
> **Currency:** 100 stotinki = 1 lev
> **Languages:** Bulgarian, Turkish
> **Religions:** Christianity, Islam (both minorities)
> **Economy:** agriculture, machinery, mining, iron, steel, wine, beer, vodka, cereals, oil, fruit and fruit products, uranium

The three-banded arrangement for this flag was adopted in 1878 when Slavic armies helped drive the Turkish occupiers out of Bulgaria; the colours are white for peace, green for freedom and red for the blood of those who attained that freedom. The national emblem was added in 1947, and has undergone modifications since. The rampant lion has been Bulgaria's symbol since the 14th century; the wheatears and the arc of a cogwheel represent, respectively, agriculture and industrialization, and the union between the workers in both spheres.

BURKINA FASO

Republic of
République de Burkina Faso

> **Population:** 9,000,000
> **Capital:** Ouagadougou
> **Population:** 235,000
> **Area:** 105,000 sq mi (275,000 km²)
> **Currency:** 100 centimes = 1 franc (CFA)
> **Languages:** French, various African languages
> **Religions:** indigenous religions, Islam, Christianity
> **Economy:** agriculture, cotton, cereals, peanuts, rubber

The red, green and yellow of this flag are the Pan-African colours, and they signify fellowship with other ex-colonial African nations. This flag was adopted in 1984, after the coup of 1983, which brought the mixed civilian-military government of Captain Thomas Sankara to power; along with the new flag came the new name of the country (which had previously been Upper Volta): Burkina Faso means "The Land of The Honest People" or "The Republic of Upright Men". Unfortunately some of the "upright men", to the dismay of the majority, in 1987 overthrew Sankara – a popular, active and reforming socialist leader – in a coup led by Captain Blaise Compaoré. The five-pointed star can be taken to symbolize either freedom or revolution.

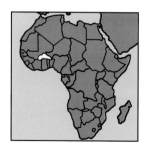

BURUNDI

Republic of
République du Burundi

> **Population:** 5,200,000
> **Capital:** Bujumbura
> **Population:** 160,000
> **Area:** 10,750 sq mi (28,000 km²)
> **Currency:** 100 centimes = 1 franc (Burundi)
> **Languages:** Kirundi, French, Swahili, Bantu
> **Religions:** Christianity (mostly RC), indigenous religions (Islam minority)
> **Economy:** agriculture, coffee, cotton, tea, fishing, wood

The colours of the Burundi flag, which reached its modern form in 1967, are white for peace, green for hope and red for the independence struggle and the sacrifices made by the people prior to the gaining of that independence in 1962. The three green-rimmed red stars stand for the three words of the national motto – "Unity, Work, Progress" – and also for the three peoples of Burundi, the Tutsi, the Hutu and the Twa. The reality of the state has belied these pacific ideals: the pygmy Twa, the country's aborigines, have virtually disappeared, and the Tutsi and the Hutu have disputed power bloodily ever since independence.

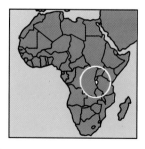

BURMA
See Myanmar

CAMBODIA

Kampuchea

Population: 7,900,000
Capital: Phnom Penh
Population: 650,000
Area: 70,000 sq mi (181,000 km²)
Currency: 100 sens = 1 riel
Languages: Khmer, French
Religions: Buddhism, Islam
Economy: agriculture, rubber, vegetables, rice

Before 1989 the flag of Cambodia featured a plain red background on which was superimposed a silhouette of the famous Angkor Wat – the main temple, dating from the early 12th century, of the ruined city of Angkor, founded in the late 9th century as capital of the Khmer Empire – with two steps on each side of five towers. The number of towers distinguished this flag, adopted in 1978 by the Vietnam-controlled puppet government of the National United Front for the Salvation of Kampuchea (as Cambodia was then known), from the very similar three-towered version flown in 1975–8 when the country was suffering under the regime of Pol Pot (1926–) and his Khmer Rouge. In 1989, with the withdrawal of the Vietnamese, the current "flag of national unity" was introduced, retaining Angkor Wat's five towers but now on a background of red and blue.

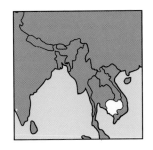

BELOW **Angkor Wat, the greatest Khmer temple in the capital Angkor, built by the King Suryavarmen during the 12th century. The silhouette of the temple is represented on the country's flag.**

CAMEROON

United Republic of
République Unie du Cameroun

Population: 10,800,000
Capital: Yaoundé
Population: 500,000
Area: 183,500 sq mi (475,400 km²)
Currency: 100 centimes = 1 franc (CFA)
Languages: French, English, local languages
Religions: Christianity, indigenous religions, Islam
Economy: agriculture, oil, gas, rubber, aluminium, vegetables

The green, red and yellow of the Cameroon flag are the Pan-African colours. The flag's form is based on the French tricolour, reflecting the fact that before 1960 the country was divided in two, the larger French Cameroon and the smaller British Cameroon. In that year the French part became the independent Cameroon Republic; in 1961 part of the British section federated with the young republic (the other part of it opted to join Nigeria), and two small yellow stars were added to the flag's central stripe. In 1972 the two parts became fully united, and the two stars became a single, larger one.

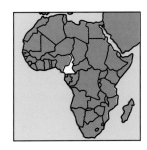

CANADA

Dominion of

Population: 26,000,000
Capital: Ottawa
Population: 738,000
Area: 3,850,350 sq mi (9,975,000 km^2)
Currency: 100 cents = 1 dollar (Canadian)
Languages: English, French
Religion: Christianity
Economy: cereals, fruit, vegetables, oil, gas, coal, metals, forestry, paper and other wood products, fish, minerals, tobacco, engineering, iron and steel, chemicals, fertilizers, machinery, automobiles

The present maple leaf flag of Canada dates from 1965. Before that, since 1892, the country had used the British Red Ensign with the Canadian arms, but the French community quite justifiably resented this symbol of an allegiance they did not feel, and so it was determined that a new, non-controversial flag should be created. Initially, at least, it succeeded in uniting the communities of Canada around a single cause: detestation of their new flag! However, the design attained its purpose: to be of a uniquely Canadian character, showing no affinities to either France or the UK. Curiously, the red verticals on either side of the maple leaf (the long-time national symbol) represent the Atlantic and Pacific oceans; they were originally intended to be blue, but altered so that the flag would accord with what had been the official colours of Canada since 1921: white for the snowy wastes of the north and red for the blood of those Canadians who had sacrificed their lives in World War I.

CANADA

Alberta

Population: 2,375,000
Capital: Edmonton
Population: 574,000
Area: 255,200 sq mi (661,200 km^2)

The ultramarine background of the provincial flag represents the Pacific Ocean. Drawn from the provincial coat of arms, the shield shows, in the foreground, stylized ears at the edge of a field of wheat that stretches across the prairie towards a distant horizon of mountains. Above is a St George's Cross, representing the province's links with England. The flag was adopted in 1968.

British Columbia

Population: 2,889,000
Capital: Victoria
Population: 66,300
Area: 366,100 sq mi (948,600 km^2)

The upper half of the provincial flag, adopted in 1960, is an elongated Union Jack with, at its centre, a crown in gold. The lower part shows an ostentatious setting sun, denoting British Columbia's status as Canada's most westerly province, against a background of wavy blue and white lines, representing the waters of the Pacific Ocean.

Manitoba

Population: 1,071,000
Capital: Winnipeg
Population: 594,600
Area: 250,900 sq mi (650,100 km^2)

Essentially this flag, adopted in 1966, is the British Red Ensign with the province's shield, showing a St George's Cross, representing the province's links with England, and, beneath it, a buffalo, symbolizing the significant role that animals played in the province's early history.

New Brunswick

Population: 710,400
Capital: Fredericton
Population: 44,400
Area: 28,400 sq mi (73,450 km^2)

The province's flag, adopted in 1965, is a somewhat stretched-out version of its coat of arms, showing a stylized lion above and a sailing ship beneath. The lion expresses the province's links with the UK, and the galley acknowledges the importance in the province's history of both seafaring and shipbuilding.

PROVINCES AND TERRITORIES

Newfoundland

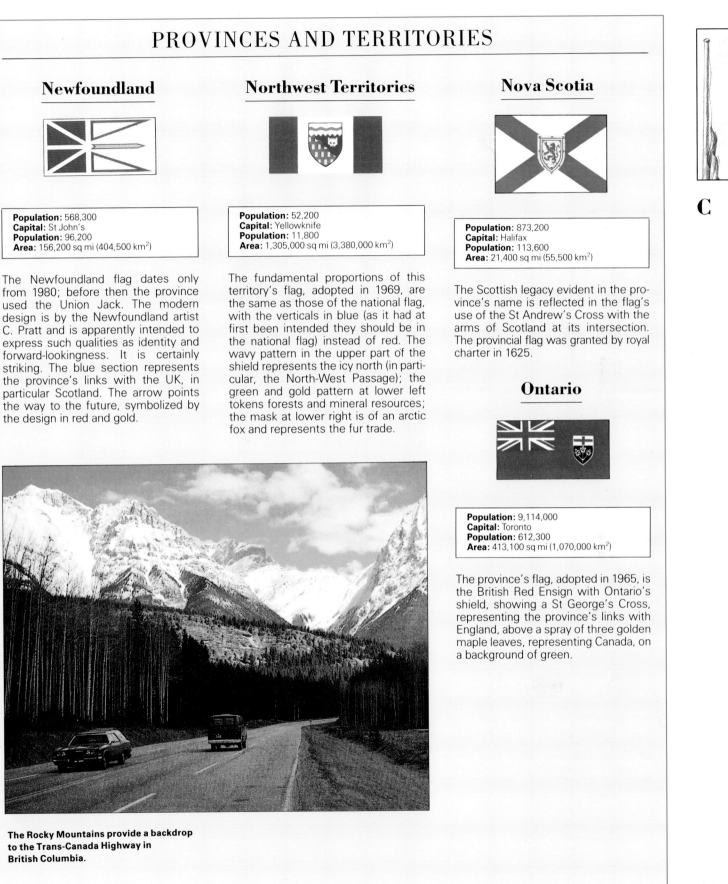

Population: 568,300
Capital: St John's
Population: 96,200
Area: 156,200 sq mi (404,500 km²)

The Newfoundland flag dates only from 1980; before then the province used the Union Jack. The modern design is by the Newfoundland artist C. Pratt and is apparently intended to express such qualities as identity and forward-lookingness. It is certainly striking. The blue section represents the province's links with the UK, in particular Scotland. The arrow points the way to the future, symbolized by the design in red and gold.

Northwest Territories

Population: 52,200
Capital: Yellowknife
Population: 11,800
Area: 1,305,000 sq mi (3,380,000 km²)

The fundamental proportions of this territory's flag, adopted in 1969, are the same as those of the national flag, with the verticals in blue (as it had at first been intended they should be in the national flag) instead of red. The wavy pattern in the upper part of the shield represents the icy north (in particular, the North-West Passage); the green and gold pattern at lower left tokens forests and mineral resources; the mask at lower right is of an arctic fox and represents the fur trade.

Nova Scotia

Population: 873,200
Capital: Halifax
Population: 113,600
Area: 21,400 sq mi (55,500 km²)

The Scottish legacy evident in the province's name is reflected in the flag's use of the St Andrew's Cross with the arms of Scotland at its intersection. The provincial flag was granted by royal charter in 1625.

Ontario

Population: 9,114,000
Capital: Toronto
Population: 612,300
Area: 413,100 sq mi (1,070,000 km²)

The province's flag, adopted in 1965, is the British Red Ensign with Ontario's shield, showing a St George's Cross, representing the province's links with England, above a spray of three golden maple leaves, representing Canada, on a background of green.

The Rocky Mountains provide a backdrop to the Trans-Canada Highway in British Columbia.

C

CANADA — PROVINCES AND TERRITORIES

Prince Edward Island

Population: 126,600
Capital: Charlottetown
Population: 15,800
Area: 2200 sq mi (5660 km²)

Where Nova Scotia (of which Prince Edward Island was a part until 1769) has a flag proudly boasting Scottishness, this flag, adopted in 1964, has a stretched English lion above a large oak tree and three young ones; the large oak is for the united purpose of Canada and the UK, and the three saplings are for the three counties of the province. The border is in red and white, the colours of St George – yet another expression of Englishness. The province was named in 1799 for Edward, Duke of Kent (1767–1820), fourth son of George III and the future father of Queen Victoria.

Quebec

Population: 6,540,000
Capital: Quebec
Population: 164,600
Area: 590,000 sq mi (1,540,700 km²)

The flags of most of the other provinces reflect Britishness, but the Quebec *Fleurdelysé* flag, adopted in 1948, is defiantly French in its use of both the fleur de lys, representing the coat of arms of the French kings (although in white rather than in the traditional French gold) and the white cross on a blue background.

Most of the remaining Inuit live in scattered settlements or reserves throughout Canada and display a Totem pole outside their homes to show rank and lineage.

The emblem of Canada, the maple leaf

C

Saskatchewan

Population: 1,010,000
Capital: Regina
Population: 175,000
Area: 251,700 sq mi (651,900 km²)

The Saskatchewan flag, adopted in 1969 (the design was a competition winner), shows the shield from the coat of arms, with a red lion (representing the UK) on a golden background above a green field with three stylized, golden sheaves (Saskatchewan is North America's most important wheat-growing region). The major image of the flag is a red prairie lily, the flower having been adopted as the province's plant-badge in 1941. The background colours are green for the province's forests and gold for her expansive fields of wheat.

Yukon Territory

Population: 23,500
Capital: Whitehorse
Population: 15,200
Area: 207,000 sq mi (536,300 km²)

The arms of the Yukon, shown in the central white strip of the flag, which was adopted in 1967, have a shield with a malamute above and a pair of fire-weed fronds beneath. The upper part of the shield shows a St George's Cross (representing the English explorers in the territory) with, at its intersection, a circle of the heraldic stylized fur called vair. The design in the lower part of the shield represents the Yukon river flowing through the province's gold-rich mountains.

CAPE VERDE

Republic of
República do Cabo Verde

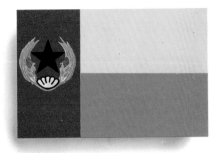

Population: 360,000
Capital: Praia
Population: 40,000
Area: 1560 sq mi (4030 km²)
Currency: 100 centavos = 1 escudo (Cape Verdean)
Languages: Portuguese, Crioulo
Religion: Christianity (mainly RC)
Economy: agriculture, fishing, coffee, sugar, canning

Although of different proportions, this flag is overall similar to that of Guinea-Bissau (*q.v.*), showing the Pan-African colours and the star symbolizing African freedom. Here, however, the star is partially framed by a garland made up of two maize sheaves, with cobs, and, at the bottom, a stylized yellow clam-shell. The similarity between the two nations' flags is explained by the fact that both are derived from that of the Partido Africano da Independencia da Guiné e Cabo Verde (PAIGC; African Party for the Independence of Guinea and Cape Verde), the liberation movement which succeeded in gaining independence for both countries (Guinea-Bissau in 1974, Cape Verde in 1975). PAIGC's aim had been that the two nations should unite, but this merger was scotched in 1980 by a military coup in Guinea-Bissau.

CAYMAN ISLANDS
See United Kingdom

CENTRAL AFRICAN REPUBLIC

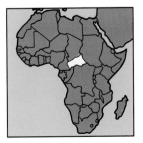

Population: 2,770,000
Capital: Bangui
Population: 388,000
Area: 240,000 sq mi (623,000 km²)
Currency: 100 centimes = 1 franc (CFA)
Languages: French, Sango
Religions: indigenous religions, Christianity (Islam minority)
Economy: agriculture, coffee, diamonds, gold, ivory, forestry

The Pan-African colours are red, yellow and green; those of the French tricolour are red, white and blue. The flag of the Central African Republic (formerly part of French Equatorial Africa) brings together both colour schemes in a single flag, with the shared red vertical stripe. The intention was to encourage a partnership between, on the one hand, a union of the Central African Republic and the other states that had once been part of French Equatorial Africa and, on the other, France herself. Such an African union — expressed by the yellow star at top left — has, of course, not come about. The flag was adopted in 1958, two years before independence; it was used unaltered during the brief period (1977–9) when Jean Bedel Bokassa (1921–), dictatorial president since a coup in 1966, declared the country an empire and himself its first emperor, Bokassa I.

CHAD

Republic of
République du Tchad

Population: 5,400,000
Capital: Ndjamena (N'Djamena)
Population: 305,000
Area: 495,700 sq mi (1,284,000 km²)
Currency: 100 centimes = 1 franc (CFA)
Languages: French, Arabic, indigenous
 languages
Religions: Islam, indigenous religions
 (Christian minority)
Economy: agriculture, cotton, beef, fishing,
 mining

Adopted in 1959, the year before independence, the flag of Chad is much like the French tricolour but with a compromise in terms of the colours used: red and blue from the French scheme and red and yellow from the Pan-African colours. The red can be taken to represent the sacrifice for freedom, yellow both the desert of the nation's north and the bright sun, and blue the clear, tropical sky.

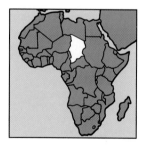

CHILE

Republic of
República de Chile

Population: 12,750,000
Capital: Santiago
Population: 4,050,000
Area: 292,270 sq mi (757,000 km²)
Currency: 1000 escudos = 1 peso
Language: Spanish
Religion: Christianity (mainly RC)
Economy: agriculture, metals, coal, paper
 and other wood products, fishing,
 wine, forestry

The Chilean flag is based on that used by the country's independence movement, which eventually succeeded in its aim on 1 January 1818. The real inspiration for both the earlier flag and the version adopted in 1818, however, seems almost certainly to have been the Stars and Stripes (which bore substantially fewer stars in those days!) – indeed, according to one version of the flag's history the creative genius behind it was that of a US national, Charles Wood, who was serving among the freedom fighters. The almost-finalized flag, without the star, was in use for a few months before being officially adopted on independence day, when the star was added. The colours are supposed to represent the blood shed by the rebels, the snow of the Andean peaks and the sky.

CHINA

People's Republic of
Zhonghua Renmin Gonghe Guo

Population: 1,105,000,000
Capital: Beijing
Population: 9,250,000
Area: 3,706,000 sq mi (9,600,000 km²)
Currency: 100 fen = 1 yuan
Languages: various forms of Chinese
 (notably Mandarin), Tibetan,
 Mongolian, Uygur, Miao, Zhuang, Yao
Religions: Buddhism, Taoism, Islam,
 Christianity (all minorities); atheism
 dominant; Confucianism outnumbers
 all religions combined
Economy: oil, gas, minerals, textiles,
 cereals, sugar, tobacco, tea, wood,
 fishing, coal, iron, minerals, machinery,
 chemicals, automobiles

This flag was introduced in 1949 on the declaration of the People's Republic of China by the triumphant communists. Red and yellow are traditional colours of China and, of course, red is also the colour of communism. The large five-pointed star represents the Communist Party's programme, while the four smaller ones are for the four sections of society that, it was claimed, would be united by and would unite to carry through that programme; the four classes were the peasantry, the workers, the bourgeoisie and those capitalists who would participate in the ongoing revolution. The similarity in the flag's basic design with that of the now defunct Union of Soviet Socialist Republics is, naturally, no coincidence.

C

CHRISTMAS ISLANDS
See Australia

COCOS ISLAND
See Australia

The arms of Colombia

COLOMBIA
Republic of
República de Colombia

Population: 30,250,000
Capital: Bogotá
Population: 4,600,000
Area: 439,800 sq mi (1,139,000 km²)
Currency: 100 centavos = 1 peso
Language: Spanish
Religion: Christianity (mainly RC)
Economy: coffee, textiles, sugar, agriculture, oil, gas, metals, emeralds, mining, machinery

---

The similarities between the flag of Colombia and those of Ecuador and Venezuela (*qq.v.*) are striking and not coincidental. These countries, along with Panama, were once the vast Spanish territory of New Granada, which was colonized in the 16th century. Simón Bolívar (1783–1830), the Liberator, secured the independence of the territory in 1819–21, and it was named Greater Colombia. The new nation did not retain its integrity very long: Ecuador and Venezuela seceded in 1830 (Panama became independent in 1903). The yellow, blue and red colours were those adopted by the Venezuelan freedom fighter Francisco de Miranda (1750–1816) to convey the message that the nation (yellow) was separated by the sea (blue) from Spain, the red seemingly indicating both the liberation of the South American territories and the blood their people were willing to shed in attaining that freedom. The current version of the Colombian flag was introduced in 1861.

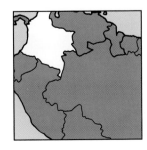

COMMONWEALTH OF INDEPENDENT STATES
(former Union of Soviet Socialist Republics)

See Armenia, Azerbaijan, Belorussia, Estonia, Georgia, Kazakhstan, Kirgizstan, Latvia, Lithuania, Moldova, Russia, Tajikistan, Turkmenia, Uzbekistan, Ukraine

COMOROS
Federal and Islamic Republic of the
République fédérale et islamique des Comores

Population: 487,000
Capital: Moroni (Njazidja)
Population: 16,000
Area: 838 sq mi (2170 km²)
Currency: 100 centimes = 1 franc (CFA)
Languages: Swahili, Arabic, French
Religion: Islam
Economy: vanilla, agriculture, fishing, perfumery

Adopted in 1978, the flag of the Comoros uses the Islamic colour green and the Islamic symbol of the crescent. The four stars symbolize the four main islands of the group, which attained independence in 1975; one of those four islands, Mayotte, in fact chose to remain a French dependency, but the number of stars was not amended – presumably in the hope that Mayotte may one day change its mind.

CONGO

People's Republic of
République populaire du Congo

Population: 1,890,000
Capital: Brazzaville
Population: 423,000
Area: 132,000 sq mi (342,000 km²)
Currency: 100 centimes = 1 franc (CFA)
Languages: French, local languages
Religions: Christianity, indigenous religions
Economy: oil, wood, agriculture, coffee, sugar, metals

The Congolese flag – adopted in 1970 when a Marxist regime was set up by Major Marien Ngouabi (d1977), who had come to power in a coup in 1968 – combines the Pan-African colours of yellow, red and green with a design based on that of the flag of the Union of Soviet Socialist Republics (see Commonwealth of Independent States), the red obviously being shared by both philosophical impulses. The crossed hoe and hammer reflect the union between peasants and industrial workers on which the country's prosperity depends; the five-pointed star denotes freedom; and the branches are a sign of peace.

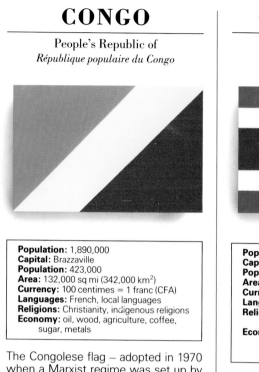

COOK ISLANDS
See New Zealand

COSTA RICA

Republic of
República de Costa Rica

Population: 2,850,000
Capital: San José
Population: 278,000
Area: 19,600 sq mi (51,000 km²)
Currency: 100 centimos = 1 colón
Language: Spanish
Religion: Christianity (almost exclusively RC)
Economy: coffee, fruit, agriculture, beef, aluminium, sugar, minerals, fishing, cocoa, textiles

Until 1821 Costa Rica was part of the captaincy-general of Guatemala, which was ruled by Spain; when the captaincy-general as a whole declared independence but was almost immediately swallowed up by the Mexican Empire. By 1824 Costa Rica, El Salvador, Guatemala, Honduras and Nicaragua – had regained their freedom and formed the Central American Federation (or United Provinces of Central America), a loosely knit arrangement that was soon to be unravelled, in 1838. The flag of the CAF was a simple blue and white triband and after the CAF's break-up these colours were adopted by Costa Rica, although in a different arrangement. In 1848 the flag was altered to include a central red stripe in honour of the ousting in that year of Louis Philippe (1773–1850) from his throne as King of the French. The arms, which do not appear in the Costa Rican civil flag, depict the rising sun of freedom, three volcanoes, seven stars (there are seven provinces) and, one on each of the Atlantic and Pacific oceans, two sailing ships.

CROATIA

Hrvatska

Population: 4,601,469
Capital: Zagreb
Population: 1,175,000
Area: 21,820 sq mi (56,550 km²)
Language: Serbo-Croat
Religion: Christianity (almostly exclusively Roman Catholic)
Economy: agriculture, bauxite, limestone, iron ore, hydroelectricity, tourism, shipping

Croatia seceded from Yugoslavia (*q.v.*) in 1991 at the end of a period of civil war that was short but on occasion extremely brutal; one reason for the brutality was that during World War II Croatia was a Nazi puppet state, and memories were still strong of atrocities allegedly committed by the Croats against their minorities, notably the Serbs, who by contrast formed the majority of the population of Yugoslavia as a whole. As a monarchy, Croatia had had a long period of stability from 1102 until 1849, being an autonomous kingdom under the Hungarian crown; it was then successively an Austrian crownland and (1868) a Hungarian crownland before the formation of Yugoslavia. At the time of writing (March 1992) there are natural but possibly unjustified fears that powerful Croatian nationalism may lead the new country down a fascist or quasi-fascist road.

CUBA

Republic of
República de Cuba

Population: 10,400,000
Capital: Havana
Population: 1,950,000
Area: 44,200 sq mi (114,500 km^2)
Currency: 100 centavos = 1 peso
Language: Spanish
Religion: Christianity (mainly RC)
Economy: agriculture, sugar, tobacco, rice, coffee, metals, fishing

The ironic similarity between the "Lone Star" flag of Cuba and the Stars and Stripes of its arch enemy, the USA, is far from coincidental. The design can be traced to 1849 and General Narcisco López (d1851), a Venezuelan filibuster who, living in the USA, was anxious to liberate Cuba from the Spanish and claim it for his adopted country – hence the single star, to be added to the others. The red triangle symbolized freedom from the Spanish and the blood that would have to be shed to attain it; the three sides represent liberty, fraternity and equality. The Spanish left the island in 1898, at which time López's design was adopted, and for three years Cuba was occupied by the USA before gaining full independence in 1901 (declared 1902). It has, of course, retained that independence since.

CYPRUS

Republic of
Kypriaki Dimokratia

Population: 700,000
Capital: Nicosia
Population: 180,000
Area: 3570 sq mi (9250 km^2)
Currency: 1000 mils = 1 pound (Cypriot)
Languages: Greek, Turkish, English
Religions: Christianity (mainly Greek Orthodox), Islam
Economy: agriculture, metals, clothing, grapes, wine, tourism, fishing

The flag of Cyprus, adopted on independence in 1960, expresses a hope rather than a reality. The declaration of independence and the adoption of the flag came after about a decade of vicious terrorism waged by the Greek Cypriots, who wished to oust the latest in a long line of occupiers, the British, in order to regain union with Greece. The large Turkish minority made such an end unthinkable, so independence was granted as a compromise. The olive branches and the white background had clear meanings of peace and harmony between the two communities, an ideal that has never been attained. Civil war continued until 1964, and in 1974 Turkey invaded to annexe part of the island for the Turkish Cypriots; since then the two parts have used the Greek and Turkish national flags, although the official flag shown here is used abroad and, occasionally, within the Greek community. The copper colouring of the central map reflects the meaning of the island's name, "Copper Isle" – Cyprus has economically viable mineral reserves of copper, chromium and iron.

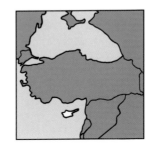

CZECHOSLOVAKIA

Česká a Slovenská Federativní Republika

Population: 15,600,000
Capital: Prague
Population: 1,200,000
Area: 49,400 sq mi (128,000 km^2)
Currency: 100 haler = 1 koruna
Languages: Czech, Slovak, Hungarian
Religion: Christianity (mainly RC)
Economy: machinery, metals, automobiles, chemicals, potatoes, coal, sugar, textiles, rolling stock

Czechoslovakia is something of a compromise country, and the colours of its flag are therefore likewise something of a compromise. The nation was formed in 1918, following the collapse of the Austrian Empire, by Edvard Beneš (1884–1948) and Tomáš Masaryk (1850–1937) out of the Austrian possessions Bohemia, Moravia and part of Silesia (Ruthenia was added in 1920). World War II effected further changes, including the loss of Ruthenia to the USSR, in 1948 communism triumphed and in 1949 the nation's two separate republics – Slovakia to the east and the Czech Socialist Republic to the west – were established. Czech and Slovak are still the two official languages. The 1918 flag was that of (Czech) Bohemia–Moravia, in red and white. The first official flag (1920) incorporated a blue triangle (smaller than the current one), to represent the Slav element of the population, red, white and blue having been the colours of the 19th-century Pan-Slavic liberation movement.

C

DENMARK

Kingdom of
Kongeriget Danmark

Population: 5,130,000
Capital: Copenhagen (København)
Population: 640,000
Area: 16,600 sq mi (43,000 km²)
Currency: 100 øre = 1 krone
Language: Danish
Religion: Christianity (almost exclusively Evangelical Lutheran)
Economy: agriculture, dairy produce, meat, poultry, engineering, shipbuilding, oil refining, electronics, furniture, chemicals

According to legend, the Danish King Valdemar II (1170–1241) had a vision on the eve of the Battle of Lyndanisse of a white crucifix in the darkening sky; this he interpreted to mean that Christ wished him to triumph in slaughtering the unfortunate Estonians on the morrow, which he duly did. Thus was born the Scandinavian Cross, seen also in the flags of Finland, Iceland, Norway and Sweden (*qq.v.*); the cross was originally square, but over the centuries one of its horizontals was extended. The red, retained in the Danish version, represents either the sullen evening sky against which Valdemar saw the cross or the blood of the succeeding battle.

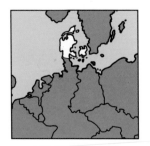

DENMARK ASSOCIATED LANDS

Faeroe Islands

Føroyar

Population: 47,000
Capital: Thorshavn
Population: 14,000
Area: 540 sq mi (1400 km²)
Economy: agriculture, fishing, canned fish, fish oil

The flag uses the Scandinavian Cross, like Denmark's. Iceland (*q.v.*) had established her own flag in 1918, and this inspired some Faroese to produce something similar, although with a different disposition of red, white and blue.

Greenland

Grønland

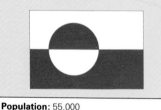

Population: 55,000
Capital: Godthåb (Nuuk)
Population: 11,000
Area: 840,000 sq mi (2,175,600 km²)
Economy: fishing, mining, furs, skins, zinc, lead

Until 1979, when Greenland was granted home rule, it used the Danish flag. Since then Danes have formed a political minority reflecting their demographic minority, and so in 1985, after extended discussion, Greenland adopted a design intended to symbolize the dawn sun and its reflection on pack-ice.

DJIBOUTI

Republic of
République de Djibouti

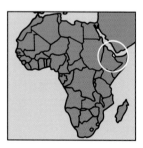

Population: 456,000
Capital: Djibouti
Population: 120,000
Area: 8880 sq mi (23,000 km²)
Currency: 100 centimes = 1 franc (Djibouti)
Languages: Arabic, French, Somali, Afar
Religion: Islam
Economy: animal husbandry, hides, skins, fishing, dates

The two ethnic groups of Djibouti are the majority Issas and the minority Afars — before gaining independence in 1977 the country was for a time known as the French Territory of the Afars and the Issas. The two groups came together in 1972 as the Popular African League for Independence (LPAI), dedicated to fighting for freedom, and adopted the current national flag, which has the traditional blue of the Issas and the traditional green of the Afars, along with white for peace and the red five-pointed star for unity.

DOMINICA

Commonwealth of

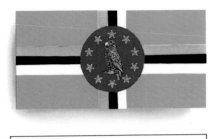

Population: 94,000
Capital: Roseau
Population: 8,400
Area: 290 sq mi (750 km²)
Currency: 100 cents = 1 dollar (East Caribbean)
Languages: English, French
Religion: Christianity (mainly RC)
Economy: bananas, coconuts, copra, fruit, cocoa, beef, soap

The device at the centre of Dominica's flag is adapted from the coat of arms, adopted in 1961 and, before the country's independence in 1978, used on the British Blue Ensign to form the national flag. The parrot is a sisserou, the national bird, a species – *Amazona imperialis* – not known outside the island. The redness of the disc is for socialism, and the ten stars surrounding the sisserou are for the island's 10 parishes. The green background represents the country's lush vegetation. The cross is of Christian origin, its tripleness symbolizing the Holy Trinity; its colours are black for the African origins of most of the population, yellow for the Carib aboriginals and white for peace and purity. Between 1978 and 1981, when the modern form was adopted, the colours of the cross were in a different order and the sisserou's posture was slightly different.

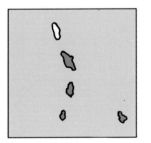

DOMINICAN REPUBLIC

República Dominicana

Population: 6,750,000
Capital: Santo Domingo
Population: 1,318,000
Area: 18,700 sq mi (48,430 km²)
Currency: 100 centavos = 1 peso
Language: Spanish
Religion: Christianity (almost exclusively RC)
Economy: agriculture, sugar, rum, tobacco, tourism, textiles, coffee, cocoa, gold, silver, nickel

Between 1822 and 1844 what is now the Dominican Republic was under the rule of conquering Haiti (*q.v.*), whose flag then had two horizontal bands, blue above and red beneath. In 1839 the liberation movement La Trinitaria amended the Haitian flag for its own use by superimposing a white cross (for sacrifice, faith, etc.) as well as 10 white stars, which vanished when independence was declared in 1844. The superimposition of the cross formed a pair of blue rectangles above a pair of red rectangles; this arrangement was later altered to the current one.

ECUADOR

Republic of
República del Ecuador

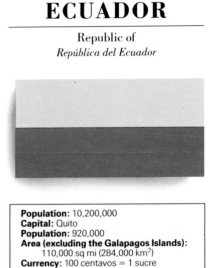

Population: 10,200,000
Capital: Quito
Population: 920,000
Area (excluding the Galapagos Islands): 110,000 sq mi (284,000 km²)
Currency: 100 centavos = 1 sucre
Languages: Spanish, indigenous languages
Religion: Christianity (almost exclusively RC)
Economy: oil, agriculture, coffee, cocoa, sugar, fruit, fishing

The story of the flag of Ecuador is much the same as that of the flag of Colombia (*q.v.*, and see also Venezuela). The yellow, blue and red colours were those adopted by the Venezuelan freedom fighter Francisco de Miranda (1750–1816) – he fought in the American Revolutionary War and the French Revolution as well as the Spanish-American Revolution – to convey the message that the nation (yellow) was separated by the sea (blue) from Spain, the red indicating both the liberation of the South American territories and the blood their people were willing to shed in attaining that freedom. The current version of the Ecuadorian flag, which is identical with the Colombian except for its narrower shape (its height:width ratio is 1:2 rather than 2:3), has been in use since 1860.

E

EGYPT

Arab Republic of
Al-Jumhūrīya Misr al-'Arabīya

Population: 52,000,000
Capital: Cairo (El Qâhira)
Population: 6,800,000
Area: 386,700 sq mi (1,001,500 km²)
Currency: 100 piastres = 1 pound (Egyptian)
Languages: Arabic, Berber, Nubian, Beja
Religion: Islam (Christian minority)
Economy: oil, gas, cotton, cereals, sugar, meat, fertilizers, textiles, fruit, vegetables, Egyptian clover

The flag of Egypt can be regarded as being in the Pan-Arab colours, like that of Jordan (*q.v.*) and others, but without the green; this is because the original flag of Egypt was itself green, and in the early years of the use of the tricolour (1952–8) the two were always flown together. In 1958, however, Egypt and Syria (*q.v.*) came together to form the United Arab Republic, with North Yemen joining a few months later. All three shared very similar flags, the Egyptian version having the two green stars still seen in the Syrian model, but with a black rather than a green band at bottom. Syria and North Yemen withdrew from the Republic almost immediately, in 1961, but Egypt continued to use the name and the flag until 1971, when she, Syria and Libya formed the Federation of Arab Republics, a loose organization almost as short-lived as its predecessor; the flag now had a golden hawk at the centre. Egypt retained the Federation flag even after 1977, when the other two countries left in disgust at Egypt's growing desire to make peace with Israel (which she effected in 1979). In 1984 the golden Eagle of Saladin, from Egypt's own arms, replaced the hawk.

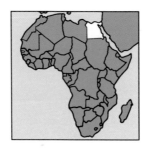

EIRE
See Ireland

EL SALVADOR

Republic of
República de El Salvador

Population: 5,200,000
Capital: San Salvador
Population: 445,000
Area: 8100 sq mi (21,000 km²)
Currency: 100 centavos = 1 colón
Languages: Spanish, indigenous languages
Religion: Christianity (almost exclusively RC)
Economy: coffee, agriculture, cotton, textiles, chemicals, sugar

Until 1821 El Salvador was part of the captaincy-general of Guatemala, which was ruled by Spain; in that year the captaincy-general as a whole declared independence but was almost immediately swallowed up by the Mexican Empire. By 1824 El Salvador and most of the other relevant provinces – notably Costa Rica, Guatemala, Honduras and Nicaragua – had regained their freedom and formed the Central American Federation (or United Provinces of Central America), a loosely knit arrangement that was soon to be unravelled, in 1838. The flag of the CAF was a simple blue and white triband, and it was to this design that El Salvador turned in 1912. The flag may be used plain, with the motto "God, Union, Liberty" or with the national arms, which show flags and, in a triangular frame, volcanoes, a rainbow (peace) and the Cap of Liberty. Compare the arms of Nicaragua (*q.v.*).

LEFT General Gamal Abdul Nasser celebrates the first anniversary of the revolution of 1952 in which King Farouk was deposed.

EQUATORIAL GUINEA

Republic of
República de Guinea Ecuatorial

Population: 420,000
Capital: Malabo
Population: 80,000
Area: 10,800 sq mi (28,000 km²)
Currency: 100 centimos = 1 ekuele
Languages: Spanish, indigenous languages
Religions: Christianity (mainly RC),
   indigenous religions
Economy: agriculture, cocoa, coffee,
   wood, fishing

Equatorial Guinea was one of the last colonial territories in Africa to gain independence, which it did in 1968 from the Spanish; it adopted its current flag at the same time. As one might expect, the green stands for agriculture, the white for peace, the red for liberation and the blue for the sea. The central emblem – altered during 1978–9, but then reinstated after a military coup that ousted (and executed) President Francisco Macias Nguema (1924–79) – is the state arms, comprising a kapok (or "God") tree with six stars above it to represent the five islands and the mainland territory that make up the nation and, below, a scroll bearing the motto *Unidad Paz Justicia* ("Unity, Peace, Justice").

ESTONIA

Population: 1,573,000
Capital: Tallinn
Population: 454,000
Area: 17,400 sq mi (45,100 km²)
Languages: Estonian, Russian
Religion: Christianity
Economy: agriculture, dairy farming,
   shipbuilding, electrical engineering,
   textiles, cement

Estonia has been a unitary state since 1991, having become so at the time of the general dissolution of the Union of Soviet Socialist Republics. During its earlier history it was ruled at various times by the Danes, the Teutonic Knights, the Swedes and the Russians. Gaining independence in 1918, it lost it again when it was annexed to the USSR in 1940, but this was not recognized by the USA, which continued to regard Estonia as illegally occupied until independence came for a second time in 1991. The climate is temperate and about one-third of the land is forested. Ethnic Estonians are related to the Finns, and this is reflected in their language, Estonian.

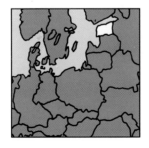

ETHIOPIA

Hybretesebawit

Population: 48,000,000
Capital: Addis Ababa
Population: 1,400,000
Area: 472,000 sq mi (1,222,000 km²)
Currency: 100 cents = 1 birr
Languages: Amharic, Galla, Arabic, Sidamo
Religions: Islam, Christianity (Coptic),
   indigenous religions
Economy: agriculture, cereals, coffee,
   cotton, sugar, textiles, hides, skins

The country has a very long history, but the story of modern Ethiopia really begins in 1941 when the fascist Italians were driven out of the land and the emperor, Haile Selassie I (1892–1977), who had earlier ruled 1930–36, was restored to the throne. His role in modernizing the country cannot be overstated, and his importance in encouraging the Pan-African cause – he played a crucial part in establishing, during the early 1960s, the Organization of African Unity (OAU) – is manifest, but was deposed by a military coup in 1974. Since then the country has been tormented by the twin and often synergistic plagues of civil war and famine. Before his coronation the emperor was Prince Ras Tafari, regarded by many as divine, and Ethiopia as a promised land; the Rastafarian religion has continued to grow in significance since his death. The Ethiopian flag, adopted in 1897 but with the colours in the reverse order, was responsible for the introduction of the Pan-African colours.

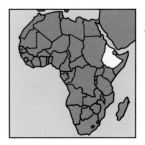

E

35

FAROE ISLANDS
See Denmark

FALKLAND ISLANDS
See United Kingdom

FIJI
State of

Population: 727,000
Capital: Suva
Population: 71,000
Area: 7100 sq mi (18,400 km²)
Currency: 100 cents = 1 dollar (Fijian)
Languages: English, Fijian, Hindustani, Tamil, Urdu, Chinese
Religions: Christianity, Hinduism, Islam
Economy: sugar, gold, agriculture, tourism, fishing, mining

The islands were discovered in 1643 by the Dutch explorer Abel Tasman (1603–59). In the late 19th century the trade in sandalwood brought many visitors to the islands, and greed-inspired rioting became rife; Fiji ceded to the UK in 1874 to bring this under control, and it was almost a century later that the state regained its independence. The flag, adopted in 1970, managed to survive the cession of Fiji to the UK, the regaining of independence and, in 1987, the departure of the nation from the Commonwealth. The design is clearly based on the British Blue Ensign, although the background shade is much paler than is customary. Also incorporated is the shield of the arms.

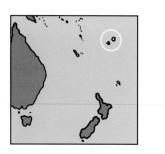

FINLAND
Republic of
Suomen Tasavalta/Republiken Finland

Population: 4,960,000
Capital: Helsinki (Helsingfors)
Population: 484,500
Area: 130,100 sq mi (337,000 km²)
Currency: 100 pennia = 1 markka
Languages: Finnish, Swedish
Religion: Christianity (mainly Lutheran)
Economy: paper and other wood products, shipbuilding, machinery, cereals, fertilizers

According to legend, the Danish King Valdemar II (1170–1241), whose lifelong hobby was conquest, had a vision on the eve of the Battle of Lyndanisse of a white crucifix in the darkening sky; this he interpreted to mean that Christ wished him to triumph in slaughter on the morrow, which he duly did. Thus was born the Scandinavian Cross, seen also in the flags of Finland, Iceland, Norway and Sweden (*qq.v.*); the cross was originally square, but over the centuries one of its horizontals was extended. The Finnish version of the standard cross – in blue and white for lakes and snowscapes – was first adopted in 1863, the same year that Finnish was recognized as the official language of the troubled country, then a part of Russia. Independence and internal strife came in 1917, and so it was not until 1919 and the establishment of the republic that the flag was once more officially adopted.

FRANCE
Republic of
République Française

Population: 55,900,000
Capital: Paris
Population: 2,200,000
Area: 212,900 sq mi (551,500 km²)
Currency: 100 centimes = 1 franc (French)
Language: French (minority tongues include Basque, Breton, Catalan, Corsican)
Religion: Christianity (mainly RC)
Economy: automobiles, engineering, metals, textiles, electrical equipment, meat, dairy produce, wine, cereals, fish, coal, oil refining, perfumery, clothing, tourism

With the Stars and Stripes, the Red Flag and the Union Jack, the French tricolor is one of the best known of all the flags of the world. The present flag dates from 1794 – the design was by Jacques-Louis David (1748–1825) at the behest of the Convention – but originated a few years earlier, in 1789, when Louis XVI (1754–93) brought the colours together by adding the blue and red of Paris to the white of the Bourbons. The flag has not been in constant use since 1794; there have been lacunae in 1814–15 and in 1815–30, and the relative widths of the stripes were varied from 1853 until legally enshrined as equal in 1946. The simple arrangement and/or the colours have inspired the flags of nations the world over.

F

FRANCE – ASSOCIATED LANDS

French Guiana
Department of
Guyane Française

Population: 90,500
Capital: Cayenne
Population: 38,150
Area: 35,100 sq mi (91,000 km²)
Economy: wood, shrimps, bauxite

French Guiana – often now referred to as Guyane – flies the French tricolour.

French Polynesia

Population: 192,000
Capital: Papeete
Population: 65,000
Area: 1540 sq mi (4000 km²)
Economy: phosphates, coconuts, copra, sugar, cotton, tourism, vanilla

Until the country gained autonomy in 1984 this flag was flown only beside the French tricolour, and its official status was debatable. The white (for idealistic purity) band is twice the width of the two red (for courage) ones. The badge (not always used) shows sun and sea, representing life and abundance, as well as a stylized depiction of a traditional dugout canoe (or pirogue), aboard which are five gesticulating oarsmen to represent the country's five island groups.

Guadeloupe and Dependencies

Population: 340,000
Capital: Basse-Terre
Population: 13,750
Area: 656 sq mi (1700 km²)
Economy: fishing, animal husbandry, furs, sealing

The flag is the French tricolour.

Martinique

Population: 335,000
Capital: Fort-de-France
Population: 101,000
Area: 425 sq mi (1100 km²)
Economy: agriculture, meat, wood, sugar, rum, tourism

The flag, which is always flown alongside the French tricolour and has dubious legal status, can be traced back to the late 18th century, when Martinique was part of the French colony St Lucia-Martinique. The L formed by the white snakes represents the name of this quondam colony but, curiously, has been retained by Martinique rather than St Lucia (*q.v*).

New Caledonia

Population: 161,000
Capital: Nouméa
Population: 60,000
Area: 7,300 sq mi (19,000 km²)
Economy: nickel, agriculture, chromium, tourism

The French tricolour is flown.

Reunion

Population: 575,000
Capital: Saint-Denis
Population: 105,000
Area: 965 sq mi (2,500 km²)
Economy: sugar, vanilla, rum, oil of geranium

The French tricolour is used.

Saint Pierre et Miquelon

Population: 6,400
Capital: Saint-Pierre
Population: 5,400
Area: 45 sq mi (240 km²)
Economy: fishing, cattle

Although widely used locally, this flag does not yet enjoy official status. The tripartile strip at left boast the department's French connections: the three panels are, from top, the Basque flag, part of the flag of Brittany and the Norman flag. The three-masted sailing ship depicted is supposed to be that of the French navigator Jacques Cartier (1491–1557), who made three voyages of discovery to North America during 1534–41, discovering this island in 1535.

Wallis and Futuna Islands

Population: 15,500
Capital: Mata-Utu
Population: 590
Area: 98 sq mi (255 km²)
Economy: coconuts, copra, fruit

This flag does not yet enjoy official status. The French tricolour at top left, separated from the rest by a thin white line, was added in 1959 when, after a referendum, the islands opted to change their status from that of protectorate to overseas territory. The square formed out of four congruent isosceles triangles represents the kings of the three main islands – Uvéa (Wallis), Futuna and Alofi – plus the French administrator.

The official seal of France; France has no arms

GABON

Republic of
République Gabonaise

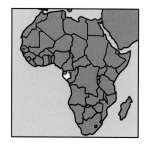

Population: 1,200,000
Capital: Libreville
Population: 350,000
Area: 103,000 sq mi (266,000 km²)
Currency: 100 centimes = 1 franc (CFA)
Languages: French, Bantu
Religions: Christianity, indigenous religions
Economy: oil, mining, agriculture, cocoa, coffee, palm oil, sugar, bananas, oil, metals

Gabon became an autonomous republic within the French Community in 1958 and gained full independence in 1960. The immediate predecessor of the modern flag was chosen in the brief interim period between the two statuses, and had the same colour scheme, although with a narrower yellow band and with the French tricolour superimposed on the green band. Today's version was adopted on independence. The green is for forestry and the blue for the Atlantic; the yellow is for both the sun and the Equator, which passes throughout Gabon.

THE GAMBIA

Republic of

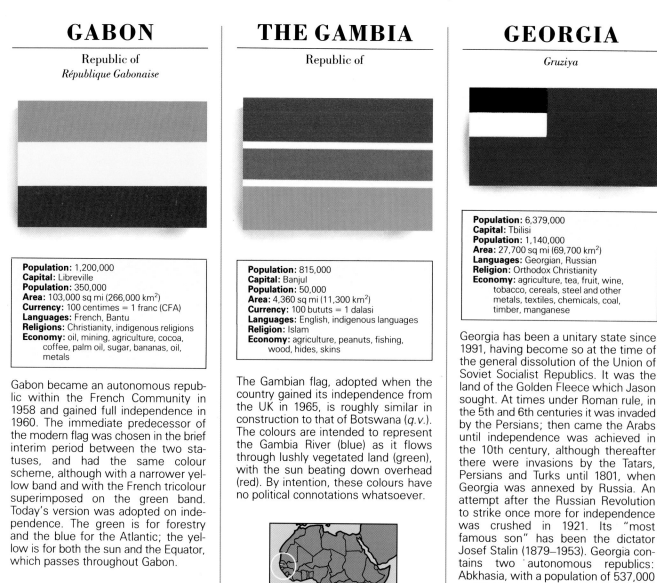

Population: 815,000
Capital: Banjul
Population: 50,000
Area: 4,360 sq mi (11,300 km²)
Currency: 100 bututs = 1 dalasi
Languages: English, indigenous languages
Religion: Islam
Economy: agriculture, peanuts, fishing, wood, hides, skins

The Gambian flag, adopted when the country gained its independence from the UK in 1965, is roughly similar in construction to that of Botswana (*q.v.*). The colours are intended to represent the Gambia River (blue) as it flows through lushly vegetated land (green), with the sun beating down overhead (red). By intention, these colours have no political connotations whatsoever.

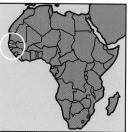

GEORGIA

Gruziya

Population: 6,379,000
Capital: Tbilisi
Population: 1,140,000
Area: 27,700 sq mi (69,700 km²)
Languages: Georgian, Russian
Religion: Orthodox Christianity
Economy: agriculture, tea, fruit, wine, tobacco, cereals, steel and other metals, textiles, chemicals, coal, timber, manganese

Georgia has been a unitary state since 1991, having become so at the time of the general dissolution of the Union of Soviet Socialist Republics. It was the land of the Golden Fleece which Jason sought. At times under Roman rule, in the 5th and 6th centuries it was invaded by the Persians; then came the Arabs until independence was achieved in the 10th century, although thereafter there were invasions by the Tatars, Persians and Turks until 1801, when Georgia was annexed by Russia. An attempt after the Russian Revolution to strike once more for independence was crushed in 1921. Its "most famous son" has been the dictator Josef Stalin (1879–1953). Georgia contains two autonomous republics: Abkhasia, with a population of 537,000 and Sukhumi as its capital, and Adzhar, with a population of 393,000 and capital Batumi.

GERMANY
Federal Republic of

Population: 76,000,000
Capital: Berlin
Population: 3,000,000
Area: 138,000 sq mi (358,000 km²)
Currency: 100 Pfennig = 1 Mark
Language: German
Religion: Christianity (Islamic minority)
Economy: machinery, precision
    instruments, rolling-stock, minerals,
    chemicals, agriculture, cereals, sugar-
    beet, coal, electrical equipment,
    electronics, computers, automobiles,
    wine, wood, food processing, fishing,
    dairy produce, oil, gas, textiles, aircraft

On reunification in 1990 to form the new Federal Republic of Germany, the former West Germany and East Germany (German Democratic Republic) opted to retain not only the West's national name but also its national flag. In fact, this flag had been used by united Germany for various periods much earlier, notably during the Weimar Republic (1919–33); it was reintroduced by both Germanies in 1949, the flag of the East differing only in that, from 1959, a communistically earnest emblem was added to the flag's centre. The colours were taken from the uniforms of the Black Jäger volunteers led against Napoleon in 1813–15 by Freiherr Ludwig von Lützow (1782–1834). When the flag was used during 1848 – the "year of revolutions" in Germany's history – the colours were romantically accorded meanings by the democratic politician and poet Ferdinand Freiligrath (1810–76) in his *Die Toten an die Lebenden:* black for gunpowder, red for blood and "the flame has a golden glow".

GHANA
Republic of

Population: 14,200,000
Capital: Accra
Population: 1,175,000
Area: 92,000 sq mi (238,500 km²)
Currency: 100 pesewas = 1 cedi
Languages: English, Akan, Ewe, Ga
Religions: Christianity, indigenous
    religions, Islam
Economy: agriculture, bauxite, cocoa,
    manganese, diamonds, gold

Ghana was the first country to adopt the Pan-African colours after they had been initiated by Ethiopia (*q.v.*); their order in the modern flag accords with that in the original Ethiopian version. The flag was adopted on Ghana's attaining independence in 1957, dropped in 1964 when the country became a one-party state – the yellow being replaced by white to match the flag of that one party, the Convention People's Party – and reintroduced in 1966. The black star represents both the people of Ghana and the cause of African unity and liberty.

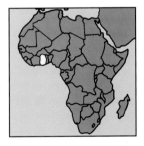

GIBRALTAR
See United Kingdom

G

LEFT **The remains of the Berlin Wall which came down in 1990 and reunited East and West Germany to form the Federal Republic of Germany.**

GREECE

Republic of
Elniki Dimokratia

Population: 10,000,000
Capital: Athens (Athínai)
Population: 886,000
Area: 51,000 sq mi (132,000 km²)
Currency: 100 lepta = 1 drachma
Language: Greek
Religion: Christianity (almost exclusively Greek Orthodox)
Economy: agriculture, fruit, cereals, tobacco, cotton, olives, grapes, wine, metals, textiles, fertilizers, chemicals, shipbuilding, tourism

The Greek flag would appear to have been inspired by the Stars and Stripes, with the stripes in this instance representing not states or districts, but the nine syllables of the freedom slogan used in the war for independence from the Ottomans during 1821–32 (trickling on after independence had, in fact, been attained in 1829), *Eleutheria i Thánatos* ("Liberty or Death"); the cross has Christian meanings that vary according to interpretation. Blue is for the sea and sky, white for the purity of the freedom fighters' cause. The shade of blue has been altered from time to time. Politics have confused the history of the national flag. Before 1970 the modern flag was, in general, flown at sea, the flag for land use showing the cross on its own; between 1970 and 1974 only the striped flag was used; in 1974–5 the two flags were used as previously; from 1975 to 1978 only the cross flag was officially used; and finally, in 1978, the current design was established as the sole national flag.

ABOVE **An aerial view of the Acropolis capped by ruins shows how this steep sided hill dominates the city of Athens, Greece.**

GREENLAND
See Denmark

GRENADA

State of

Population: 104,000
Capital: St George's
Population: 31,000
Area: 133 sq mi (345 km²)
Currency: 100 cents = 1 dollar (East Caribbean)
Languages: English, French
Religion: Christianity
Economy: agriculture, cocoa, tourism, mace and nutmeg

The flag of Grenada was adopted on the attainment of independence from the UK in 1974 and has remained unchanged. Set within the triangle to the left of centre is a stylized nutmeg, acknowledging the importance of the spice to the nation's economy. The green of the flag represents vegetal richness, the red has its customary implications of vitality, determination and liberation and the yellow is for sunshine, friendliness and wisdom. There are seven stars for the nation's seven parishes, one of which comprises those few of the Grenadine Islands that are not part of St Vincent and The Grenadines (*q.v.*); the star-shape itself expresses optimism and idealism.

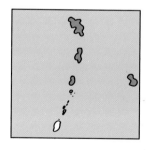

GUADELOPE AND DEPENDENCIES
See France

GUAM

See United States of America

GUATEMALA

Republic of
República de Guatemala

Population: 8,700,000
Capital: Guatemala City
Population: 755,000
Area: 42,000 sq mi (109,000 km²)
Currency: 100 centavos = 1 quetzal
Languages: Spanish, indigenous languages
Religions: Christianity (mainly RC),
   indigenous religions
Economy: coffee, oil, bananas,
   pharmaceuticals, cotton, sugar,
   tobacco, metals

Until 1821 Guatemala was part of the captaincy-general of Guatemala, which was ruled by Spain; in this year the captaincy-general as a whole declared independence, but was almost immediately swallowed up by the Mexican Empire. By 1824 Guatemala, Costa Rica, El Salvador, Honduras and Nicaragua – had regained their freedom and formed the Central American Federation, an arrangement that was soon to be unravelled, in 1838. The flag of the CAF was a simple blue and white triband, and it was to this design that Guatemala turned. Between 1851 and 1871 there were additional stripes of yellow and red; when these disappeared and the country reverted to the simple blue and white, the stripes were set vertically.

GUINEA

People's Republic of
République de Guinée

Population: 5,100,000
Capital: Conakry
Population: 763,000
Area: 95,000 sq mi (246,000 km²)
Currency: 100 kori = 1 syli
Languages: French, indigenous languages
Religions: Islam, indigenous religions
Economy: bauxite, agriculture, diamonds

The flag of Guinea, introduced a few weeks after independence in 1958, has the design of the French tricolour but using the Pan-African colours. These were adopted in imitation not of Ethiopia (*q.v.*) but of Ghana (*q.v.*), it being at the time the aim of the two countries to unite. The national motto is *Travail, Justice, Solidarité* ("Work, Justice, Solidarity"), and the red, yellow and green of the flag are sometimes taken to represent these three qualities respectively.

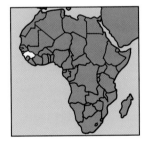

GUINEA-BISSAU

Republic of
República da Guiné-Bissau

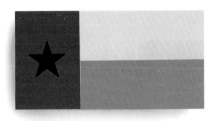

Population: 945,000
Capital: Bissau
Population: 110,000
Area: 13,900 sq mi (36,125 km²)
Currency: 100 centavos = 1 peso
Languages: Portuguese, Creole,
   indigenous languages
Religions: indigenous religions, Islam
   (Christian minority)
Economy: agriculture, fishing, palm
   kernels, cereals, wood, peanuts

Although of different proportions, this flag is overall similar to that of Cape Verde (*q.v.*), showing the Pan-African colours of red, yellow and green and the black five-pointed star symbolizing African freedom. The similarity between the two nations' flags is explained by the fact that both are derived from that of the Partido Africano da Independencia da Guiné e Cabo Verde (PAIGC; African Party for the Independence of Guinea and Cape Verde), the liberation movement that succeeded in gaining independence for both countries (Guinea-Bissau in 1974, Cape Verde in 1975). PAIGC's aim had been that the two nations should unite, and this merger was well under way when scotched in 1980 by a military coup in Guinea-Bissau.

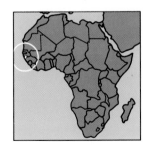

G

GUYANA

Cooperative Republic of

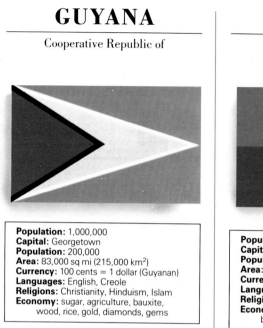

Population: 1,000,000
Capital: Georgetown
Population: 200,000
Area: 83,000 sq mi (215,000 km²)
Currency: 100 cents = 1 dollar (Guyanan)
Languages: English, Creole
Religions: Christianity, Hinduism, Islam
Economy: sugar, agriculture, bauxite, wood, rice, gold, diamonds, gems

The flag of Guyana was adopted on the country's attainment of independence from the UK in 1966; it was based on a design supplied by Dr Whitney Smith (1940–), Director of the Flag Research Center at Winchester, Massachusetts. Dr Smith has explained it as follows: "The red triangle stands for the people's zeal in nation building; its black border is for endurance. The gold arrowhead represents progress and the nation's mineral wealth; its white border is for the rivers of Guyana. The green field represents farms and forests."

The flag of the President of Guyana

GUYANE

See France

HAITI

Republic of
République d'Haiti

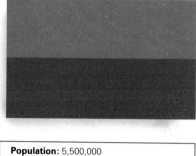

Population: 5,500,000
Capital: Port-au-Prince
Population: 690,000
Area: 10,710 sq mi (27,750 km²)
Currency: 100 centimes = 1 gourde
Languages: French, Creole
Religions: Christianity (mainly RC), Voodoo
Economy: coffee, agriculture, sugar, bauxite, sisal

The first flag of Haiti was the French tricolour, the rebelling slaves identifying with the sansculottes. On independence in 1804 Jean Jacques Dessalines (c1758–1806) became emperor and adopted a bi-colour as national flag, disposing of the white, with the blue being replaced by black. In 1806 Dessalines was assassinated and the new president of the country, Alexandre Sabès Pétion (1770–1818), reintroduced blue and red, although in part of the country only. In 1818, when Jean-Pierre Boyer (1776–1850) came to power, the pattern of two horizontal bands in blue and in red was adopted for the national flag; from 1844 the arms, in a rectangular white frame, were added. In 1964, when François Duvalier (1907–71), Papa Doc declared himself president for life, the flag was altered back to the Dessalines pattern, although the arms were retained. After Duvalier died in 1971 his son Jean-Claude Duvalier (1951–), Baby Doc, ruled in his dead father's stead until being ousted in 1986, at which point the pre-Duvalier blue and red flag was reintroduced, and is still the national flag at the time o₁ writing, in the wake of the 1991 deposition of President Jean-Bertrand Aristide.

HONDURAS

Republic of
República de Honduras

Population: 4,800,000
Capital: Tegucigalpa
Population: 510,000
Area: 43,250 sq mi (112,000 km²)
Currency: 100 centavos = 1 lempira
Languages: Spanish, indigenous languages
Religion: Christianity (almost exclusively RC)
Economy: agriculture, bananas, coffee, meat, tobacco, wood, fishing, metals

Until 1821 Honduras was part of the captaincy-general of Guatemala, which was ruled by Spain; in that year the captaincy-general as a whole declared independence but was almost immediately swallowed up by the Mexican Empire. By 1824 Honduras, Costa Rica, El Salvador, Guatemala and Nicaragua – had regained their freedom and formed the Central American Federation, a loosely knit arrangement that was soon to be unravelled, in 1838. The flag of the CAF was a simple blue and white triband, and it was to this design that Honduras turned, adding the five stars for the five CAF countries in 1866 (although this was not ratified until 1949). On the state flag the stars are differently arranged – into an arc – to accommodate the arms.

HONG KONG

See United Kingdom

HUNGARY

People's Republic of
Magyar Köztársaság

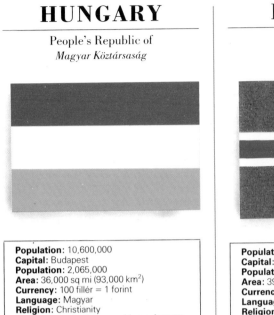

Population: 10,600,000
Capital: Budapest
Population: 2,065,000
Area: 36,000 sq mi (93,000 km²)
Currency: 100 fillér = 1 forint
Language: Magyar
Religion: Christianity
Economy: agriculture, machinery, forestry,
    wine, bauxite, coal, oil, gas, sugar,
    fruit, potatoes, automobiles, clothing

The red, white and green colours of Hungary are thought to date back to the 9th century; a precursor of the modern flag was used by King Matthias II (1557–1619), later (from 1612) Holy Roman Emperor. In 1848 the Hungarians, led by Lajos (Louis) Kossuth (1802–94), rebelled against Austrian rule and gained short-lived independence in 1849, with Kossuth as governor; he used the traditional colours in the pattern of the French tricolour, and this was thereafter the national flag with the addition of the arms, until 1945 and the declaration of a new republic. When the communists took over in 1949 they added their emblem to the flag; this was dropped in 1956 around the time of the Hungarian uprising and its brutal suppression by Soviet troops.

RIGHT **Anti-communist forces burning a portrait of Stalin during the 1956 Hungarian uprising which was eventually crushed by Soviet troops.**

ICELAND

Republic of
Lýdveldid Island

Population: 250,000
Capital: Reykjavik
Population: 87,000
Area: 39,700 sq mi (103,000 km²)
Currency: 100 aurars = 1 krona
Language: Icelandic
Religion: Christianity (almost exclusively
    Evangelical Lutheran)
Economy: fishing, agriculture, dairy
    produce, aluminium, wool, sheepskin

According to legend, the Danish King Valdemar II (1170–1241), whose life-long hobby was conquest, had a vision on the eve of the Battle of Lyndanisse of a white crucifix in the darkening sky; this he interpreted to mean that Christ wished him to triumph in slaughter on the morrow, which he duly did. Thus, so the story continues, was born the Scandinavian Cross, seen also in the flags of Finland (*q.v.*), Iceland, Norway and Sweden (*qq.v.*); the cross was originally square, but over the centuries one of its horizontals was extended. In the Icelandic version the colours reflect those of Denmark – which ruled the country 1381–1918 and of which Iceland was then an independent state until independence in 1944 – and of Norway, which ruled Iceland from 1264 until both came under the Danish crown in 1381. The Icelandic flag was adopted in 1915, but only for home waters until 1918.

I

INDIA

Republic of
Bharat

Population: 813,000,000
Capital: New Delhi
Population: 5,750,000
Area: 1,270,000 sq mi (3,288,000 km²)
Currency: 100 paise = 1 rupee
Languages: Hindi, English, Urdu and many
　　　others
Religions: Hinduism, Islam (Christian, Sikh,
　　　Buddhist and Jain minorities)
Economy: agriculture, textiles, tea, cotton,
　　　peanuts, jute, coal, oil, gas, bauxite,
　　　metals, gems, machinery

The Indian flag is very similar to that of the Indian National Congress party, from which it was directly derived. The Congress flag was first used with the colours saffron (courage and sacrifice), green (faith, fertility and chivalry) and white (truth and peace) in 1933; in the centre of the white band was the emblem of a spinning-wheel. On independence the spinning-wheel was replaced by the image of a Buddhist *dharma chakra* (wheel of life), which had recently been discovered at Sarnath on a column dating from the time of the Indian Emperor Ashoka (reigned 269–232BC), who was converted to Buddhism and established it as the state religion.

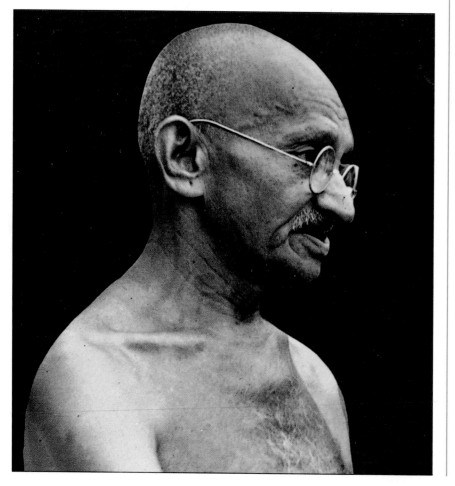

INDONESIA

Republic of
Republik Indonesia

Population: 175,000,000
Capital: Jakarta (Djakarta)
Population: 7,600,000
Area: 782,500 sq mi (2,030,000 km²)
Currency: 100 sens = 1 rupiah
Language: Bahasa Indonesian
Religions: Islam, Christianity (Hindu and
　　　Buddhist minorities)
Economy: oil, gas, wood, rubber,
　　　agriculture, sugar, palm oil, copra,
　　　coffee, tea, peanuts, fish, metals, coal,
　　　textiles, paper

Immediately after World War II, Indonesia unilaterally declared her independence from her Dutch overlords, a decision finally ratified four years later, in 1949. The national flag dates from the initial declaration of independence, its status having been confirmed in 1949. Before that it had been used from about 1924 by Indonesian freedom fighters in their struggle against the Dutch, but the use of the colours can be traced back to the 13th century. The white is, as ever, for purity and justice; the red is for gallantry and freedom. Except in its proportions, the flag is identical with the much more venerable flag of Monaco (*q.v.*).

IRAN

Islamic Republic of
Jomhori-e-Islami-e-Irân

Population: 52,500,000
Capital: Tehran (Teheran)
Population: 5,735,000
Area: 636,300 sq mi (1,648,000 km²)
Currency: 100 dinars = 1 rial
Languages: Farsi, Kurdish, Baluchi
Religion: Islam
Economy: oil, gas, textiles, rugs, agriculture, metals, coal, cotton, fruit, electrical equipment

The current form of the Iranian flag was adopted after 1979 when Shah Mohammad Reza Pahlavi (1919–80) was expelled from the country and an Islamic republic declared with the return to eminence of the Ayatollah Ruhollah Khomeini (1900–89). The colours of the flag, which was adopted in straight-forward tricolour form in 1907, are traditional, having been used on Iranian flags since at least the 18th century. The central emblem – a sword with beckoning crescents – was confirmed a little over a year after Iran's 1979 declaration of herself as a republic; it expresses Islamic values, and can be interpreted to imply the only true road to Allah. Along the edges of both the red and the green band the expression *Allah o Akbar* ("God is Great") is re-peated 22 times in all; this inscription was added at the same time as the emblem to mark the return of Khomeini to Iran on the 22nd day of the Islamic month of Bahman. Note the curious notched effect along the borders of the white stripe.

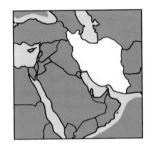

IRAQ

Republic of
al Jumhouriya al'Iraqia

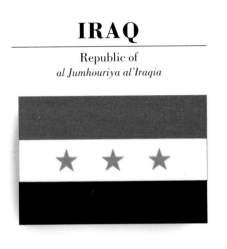

Population: 17,000,000
Capital: Baghdad
Population: 3,200,000
Area: 168,000 sq mi (435,000 km²)
Currency: 100 fils = 1 dinar
Languages: Arabic, Kurdish, Turkish, Assyrian
Religions: Islam, Christianity
Economy: oil, cotton, dates

Like that of Jordan (*q.v.*) and others, the flag of Iraq is in the Pan-Arab colours; indeed, before 1958 the Iraqi flag was hard to tell from the Jordanian, the only differences being that the red area was a trapezium rather than a tri-angle and that there were two white stars rather than one within this area. A different flag was used between 1958 (when the monarchy was ousted) and 1963, when the current flag was adopted, the three green stars repre-senting the unfulfilled expectation of coming together in political union with Egypt and Syria. Since the Gulf War of 1991, when both Egypt and Syria played an active part in the UN force that bloodily drove Iraq back out of Kuwait, such union has seemed even more remote than before.

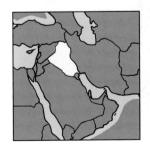

LEFT The return of Ayatollah Ruhollah Khomeini to Iran in August 1979 signalled the end of the rule by the Shah and the inception of religious rule by Muslim clerics. Iran was then declared an Islamic Republic.

IRELAND

Republic of
Éire

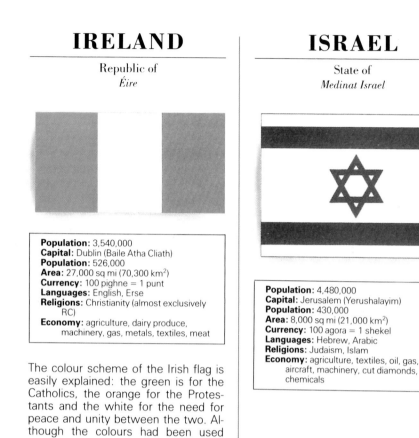

Population: 3,540,000
Capital: Dublin (Baile Atha Cliath)
Population: 526,000
Area: 27,000 sq mi (70,300 km²)
Currency: 100 pighne = 1 punt
Languages: English, Erse
Religions: Christianity (almost exclusively RC)
Economy: agriculture, dairy produce, machinery, gas, metals, textiles, meat

The colour scheme of the Irish flag is easily explained: the green is for the Catholics, the orange for the Protestants and the white for the need for peace and unity between the two. Although the colours had been used before in this way, the first significant occasion of their use was in the wake of the revolutions that swept Europe in 1848 against post-Napoleonic conservatism, resulting notably in the ousting of the French King Louis-Philippe. Even so, it was not until the 1916 uprising that the use of the colours to symbolize a free and united Ireland became widespread. The colours were formally adopted when the Irish Free State was established in 1919, and their modern arrangement was finalized in 1920. The flag has remained unchanged since.

ISRAEL

State of
Medinat Israel

Population: 4,480,000
Capital: Jerusalem (Yerushalayim)
Population: 430,000
Area: 8,000 sq mi (21,000 km²)
Currency: 100 agora = 1 shekel
Languages: Hebrew, Arabic
Religions: Judaism, Islam
Economy: agriculture, textiles, oil, gas, aircraft, machinery, cut diamonds, chemicals

Israel has had the same flag since the state was formed in 1948. The flag itself dates back to the early days of the Zionist movement, being introduced in 1891 and confirmed in 1897 by the First Zionist Congress, when the movement also established the World Zionist Organization and appointed its leading light, the Hungarian-born journalist and playwright Theodor Herzl (1860–1904), as its first president. The emblem in the centre of the flag is the Star (or Shield) of David, a six-pointed star composed of two equilateral triangles, a centuries-old Jewish symbol. Blue and white are traditional colours for ritual cloths, most especially prayer shawls, the blue stripes around the edges of which are referred to by the blue stripes in the flag.

ABOVE **Israel's first Independence Day Parade, Jerusalem, 1949. The flag of Israel was formally adopted the previous year.**

ITALY

Republic of
Repubblica Italiana

Population: 57,500,000
Capital: Rome (Roma)
Population: 2,827,000
Area: 116,300 sq mi (301,225 km²)
Currency: 100 centesimi = 1 lira
Language: Italian
Religion: Christianity (mainly RC)
Economy: agriculture, machinery, automobiles, clothing, food, textiles, footwear, wine, olives, metals

The Italian tricolour is the French tricolour but with green in place of blue. According to one legend, the change was effected because green was Napoleon's favourite colour. It first appeared in the French republics in northern Italy set up in the late 18th century, being adopted in 1797–8 by the Cisalpine Republic. In 1802 it became the flag of the Italian republic that the French had set up, and it endured until 1814. In 1848 Piedmont unsuccessfully attempted to thrust the Austians out of Lombardy, as a consequence the king of Sardinia-Piedmont, Charles Albert (1798–1849), immediately abdicated in favour of his son, Victor Emmanuel II (1820–78). Charles Albert had already, in 1848, adopted the green-white-red tricolour with the arms of the House of Savoy in the centre. In 1946, when Italy proclaimed itself a republic in the wake of World War II – its last king, Umberto II (1904–) having abdicated following a referendum that rejected the monarchy – the arms of the House of Savoy were removed.

IVORY COAST

Republic of
République de Côte d'Ivoire

Population: 11,600,000
Capitals: Abidjan (pop 1,600,000) and Yamoussoukro (pop 80,000)
Area: 125,000 sq mi (322,500 km²)
Currency: 100 centimes = 1 franc (CFA)
Languages: French, indigenous languages including Dioula
Religions: Animism, Islam, Christianity
Economy: agriculture, cocoa, coffee, cotton, wood

The flag of the Ivory Coast (or, since 1986, officially Côte d'Ivoire) was adopted in 1959, the year before the country gained its independence from France. Unlike most other ex-colonies, it decided to express in its flag its continuing relationship with its one-time ruler, adopting the pattern of the French tricolour. The sharing of colours with Ireland (*q.v.*) is coincidental. The orange is for the Ivory Coast's northern savannas, the green for its lush coastal regions and the white for the harmony and unity of these two areas.

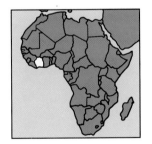

JAMAICA

State of

Population: 2,400,000
Capital: Kingston
Population: 566,000
Area: 4250 sq mi (11,000 km²)
Currency: 100 cents = 1 dollar (Jamaican)
Language: English
Religions: Christianity, Rastafarianism
Economy: sugar, coffee, bananas, bauxite, rum, tobacco

The flag of Jamaica was introduced on independence in 1962 and has remained unchanged. The design appears to have been inspired purely by aesthetics. The colours are interpreted as follows: yellow for mineral resources and for sunshine, green for agricultural wealth and for hope, and black for the hardships that the nation's people have faced in the past (notably slavery) and still continue to face.

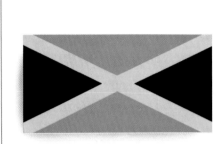

J

The arms of Jamaica

47

JAPAN

Nihon/Nippon

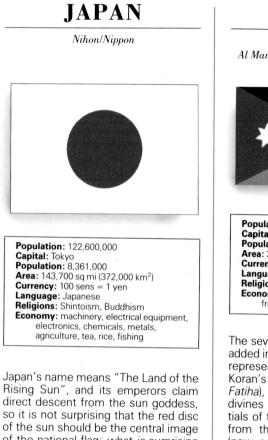

Population: 122,600,000
Capital: Tokyo
Population: 8,361,000
Area: 143,700 sq mi (372,000 km²)
Currency: 100 sens = 1 yen
Language: Japanese
Religions: Shintoism, Buddhism
Economy: machinery, electrical equipment, electronics, chemicals, metals, agriculture, tea, rice, fishing

Japan's name means "The Land of the Rising Sun", and its emperors claim direct descent from the sun goddess, so it is not surprising that the red disc of the sun should be the central image of the national flag; what *is* surprising is that this been so only since 1870 – although it had been put to mercantile use for a number of years before that, and the symbol and its imperial connections date back a further 500 years. The redness of the disc expresses qualities such as sincerity and passion, the whiteness of the background honesty and purity.

JORDAN

Hashemite Kingdom of
Al Mamiaka al Urduniya al Hashemiyah

Population: 3,940,000
Capital: Amman
Population: 744,000
Area: 37,750 sq mi (97,750 km²)
Currency: 1000 fils = 1 dinar
Language: Arabic
Religion: Islam (Christianity minority)
Economy: agriculture, minerals, chemicals, fruit, vegetables

The seven-pointed star in Jordan's flag, added in 1928 to a flag created in 1921, represents the seven verses of the Koran's first *sura*, "The Opening" (*al-Fatiha*), which is held by many Islamic divines to comprehend all the essentials of their belief. The colours derive from that of the kingdom of Hejaz (now a part of Saudi Arabia), within whose domain .lay Mecca. Before Jordan became an independent kingdom (1946) it was controlled by the UK under a League of Nations mandate and was called Transjordan; the drive for the liberation of Transjordan and other Hashemite realms of the region was inspired by Hussein ibn Ali (1856–1931), King of Hejaz, and his colours (red, white, green and black) were widely used, becoming known as the Pan-Arab colours and now adopted by a number of other Arab countries. A further reason for Jordan to take the Hejaz flag on independence in 1946 was that the new kingdom's first king, Abdullah ibn Hussein (1882–1951), was Hussein ibn Ali's second son.

KAMPUCHEA
See Cambodia

KAZAKHSTAN

Kazak

Population: 15,858,000
Capital: Alma-Ata
Population: 1,046,000
Area: 1,049,150 sq mi (2,717,300 km²)
Languages: Russian, Ukrainian, Kazakh
Religions: Christianity, Islam
Economy: wheat, cotton, fruit, coal, iron, lead, minerals, chemicals, food processing, metal processing, space science/technology/engineering (Baykonyr was the principal Soviet rocket- and missile-testing site, and most of the USSR's space vehicles have been launched from here)

Kazakhstan has been a unitary state since 1991, having become so at the time of the general dissolution of the Union of Soviet Socialist Republics. About 100 nationalities are represented in the Kazakhstani population, of whom only about one-third are native Kazakhs, adherents of Islam noted for their skill in horsemanship; most of the remaining people are either Russian or Ukrainian. The region became a part of Russia progressively through the 18th and 19th centuries; traditionally there has been rivalry over the border it shares with northwestern China.

KENYA

Republic of
Jamhuri ya Kenya

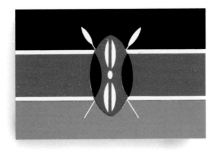

Population: 23,900,000
Capital: Nairobi
Population: 1,335,000
Area: 225,000 sq mi (583,000 km^2)
Currency: 100 cents = 1 shilling (Kenyan)
Languages: Swahili, English
Religions: Christianity, indigenous religions
(Islamic minority)
Economy: coffee, tea, oil, agriculture,
cotton, tourism

The current Kenyan flag, adopted on the country's attainment of independence from the UK in 1963, is based on that adopted in 1952 by the leading political party, the Kenya African National Union (KANU); for the national flag the central image of the Masai shield with crossed spears was elaborated and, more significantly, white stripes were added to either edge of the red band as a recognition of Kenya's other main political party, the Kenya African Democratic Union (KADU), which was soon absorbed by KANU as Kenya became a one-party state under Jomo Kenyatta (*c*1891–1978), leader of KANU from 1960 and first President of Kenya from 1964 until his death; since then little has changed under his successor, Daniel Arap Moi (1924–). Apart from the white, which implies peace and unity, the colours are those used elsewhere to express the Black liberation struggle; the weapons imply the country's will to defend its freedom.

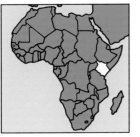

K

ABOVE **President Jomo Kenyatta addresses the crowds at Independence Day celebrations in 1963. The current Kenyan flag was adopted in the same year.**

KIRGIZSTAN

Kirghiz Republic
Kirghizia

Population: 3,976,000
Capital: Frunze
Population: 590,000
Area: 76,640 sq mi (198,500 km²)
Languages: Kirgiz, Turkish, Russian
Religion: Islam
Economy: sheep, wheat, corn, cotton, sugarbeet, tobacco, fruit, silk, coal, agricultural machinery, textiles, food processing, engineering, sawmilling

Kirgizstan has been a unitary state since 1991, having become so at the time of the general dissolution of the Union of Soviet Socialist Republics. Traditionally there has been rivalry over its border with northwestern China, where rise the vast peaks of the Tien Shan Range. There are strong links with the neighbouring, and much larger, state of Kazakhstan.

KIRIBATI

Republic of

Population: 66,250
Capital: Tarawa
Population: 17,200
Area: 264 sq mi (680 km²)
Currency: 100 cents = 1 dollar (Australian)
Languages: Gilbertese, English
Religion: Christianity
Economy: copra, handicrafts, fishing, postage stamps, coconuts

Before independence in 1979, the Gilbert Islands (as Kiribati then was) flew the British Blue Ensign with the shield from the arms of the Gilbert and Ellice Islands Protectorate, as did the Ellice Islands, now Tuvalu (*q.v.*), from which the Gilberts had been partitioned in 1975. Those arms had been granted in 1937; they showed a yellow frigate bird above a sun rising over the Pacific Ocean, and the Kiribati flag – chosen as the winner of a design competition – was drawn almost directly from them.

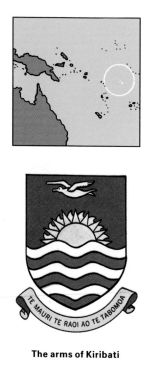

The arms of Kiribati

KOREA (North)

People's Democratic Republic of
Chosun Minchu-chui Inmin Konghwa-guk

Population: 22,000,000
Capital: Pyongyang (Pyeongyang)
Population: 1,300,000
Area: 47,350 sq mi (122,600 km²)
Currency: 100 chon = 1 won (North Korean)
Language: Korean
Religions: Shamanism, Chundo Kyo, Buddhism
Economy: agriculture, metals, chemicals

The whole of the ancient kingdom of Korea became a Japanese protectorate in 1905 and was formally annexed by Japan in 1910. After World War II the country was divided by the Allies at the 38th parallel, the north being allotted to the USSR and the south to the USA. In 1948 the north became an independent "people's democratic republic" – i.e., a communist state – and the south was established as what proved to be an equally illusory democracy. The traditional Korean flag was in the colours red, white and blue. The communist regime of the north retained these colours but expanded the red at the expense of the white and also incorporated a red star in a white disc, likewise an expression of the glorious future that communism would bring. White is for purity and the sovereignty of the nation, while blue is the desire for peace – that endured until 1950.

KOREA (South)

Republic of
Han Kook

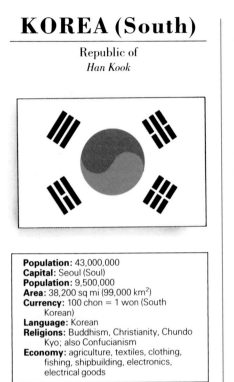

Population: 43,000,000
Capital: Seoul (Soul)
Population: 9,500,000
Area: 38,200 sq mi (99,000 km²)
Currency: 100 chon = 1 won (South Korean)
Language: Korean
Religions: Buddhism, Christianity, Chundo Kyo; also Confucianism
Economy: agriculture, textiles, clothing, fishing, shipbuilding, electronics, electrical goods

In 1948 when Korea was divided up (see North Korea) the south was established as a democracy. The traditional Korean flag was in the colours red, white and blue, and a version of it adopted in the 1880s was reintroduced in 1948, with minor adjustments, in 1950 as the flag of the south (further minor adjustments were made in 1984). The central feature is the yin-yang symbol, which has its customary Buddhist fusion-of-opposites meaning, stressed also by the choice of the colours red and blue. The white background expresses purity. The meanings of the four black trigrams fall into three sequences. Reading in each case clockwise from upper left, these are: summer, autumn, winter, spring; south, west, north, east; sky (heaven), moon, Earth, sun.

KUWAIT

State of
Dowlat al Kuwayt

Population: 2,000,000
Capital: Kuwait City (Al-Kuwayt)
Population: 182,000
Area: 6875 sq mi (17,800 km²)
Currency: 1000 fils = 1 dinar
Languages: Arabic, English
Religion: Islam
Economy: oil, gas, agriculture, fishing, desalination

Like that of Jordan (*q.v.*) and others, the Kuwaiti flag is in the Pan-Arab colours of red, white, green and black. The flag was adopted in 1961, when Kuwait gained its independence from the UK, of which it had been a protectorate since 1914. (In fact, UK troops had to be called back almost immediately after independence, as Iraq threatened to annexe the fledgling nation. Another attempt in 1990 was bloodily repelled by a combined UN force.) There are various interpretations of the colours: red may be the blood of enemies, courage or a representation of the Hashemites; white may be purity, peace, honour or a representation of the Umayyads; green may be agriculture, vegetation or a representation of the Fatimids; and black may be colour of the future for the state's foes, the stained mud kicked up by horses in battle or a representation of the Abbasids.

The arms of Kuwait

K

The arms of the Federation of Arab Republics, 1972

LAOS

People's Democratic Republic of
Sa Thalanalath Pasathiparay Pasason Lao

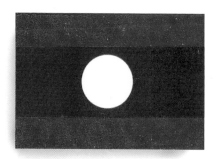

Population: 3,900,000
Capital: Vientiane (Viangchan)
Population: 300,000
Area: 91,400 sq mi (236,750 km²)
Currency: 100 ats = 1 kip
Languages: Lao, indigenous languages
Religions: Buddhism, indigenous religions, Christianity
Economy: agriculture, wood, coffee, cotton, tobacco, tin

In 1954 Laos attained its full independence from the French, but the country remained a constitutional monarchy (as it had been since 1947); at the time of independence it was already in the grip of a vicious civil war, begun in 1953, between the existing government (funded in large part by the USA and aided by great numbers of mercenaries from neighbouring Thailand) and the communist-led and Vietnam-assisted Neo Lao Istala (Laotian Patriotic Front or Pathet Lao). After an attempt at compromise government from 1974, in 1975 the Neo Lao Istala took power and declared the People's Democratic Republic of Laos. The new national flag was identical with that adopted in 1945 by the Neo Lao Istala and depicts a white (for justice and the promise of the future) full moon superimposed on a blue (for the people's well-being) Mekong River flanked on either side by red (for the unity and purpose of the Laotians and for the blood they shed during the struggle for freedom).

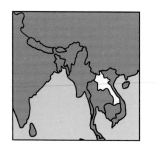

LATVIA

Latviya/Lettland

Population: 2,681,000
Capital: Riga
Population: 875,000
Area: 24,580 sq mi (63,700 km²)
Languages: Lettish, Russian, many others
Religion: Lutheran Christianity
Economy: forestry, fishing, livestock, textiles, machinery, electrical appliances, chemicals, paper, foodstuffs, furniture, steel, shipbuilding, engineering, cement, fertilizers

Latvia has been a unitary state since 1991, having become so at the time of the general dissolution of the Union of Soviet Socialist Republics; before that, since its annexation by the USSR in 1944, it was regarded by the USA and a few other Western governments as being illegally occupied. Its earlier history is virtually a string of occupations by some foreign power or another: the Vikings, Denmark, Lithuania, Germany, Poland, Sweden, Russia and the USSR — although it did have a shaky period of independence from 1920 until Russia invaded in 1940 and then Germany in 1941–4. The majority of the people are of the Letts, an ancient Baltic people, but a sizeable majority — about one-third — are Russians.

LEBANON

al-Jumhouriya al-Lubnaniya

Population: 2,600,000
Capital: Beirut
Population: 750,000
Area: 4,000 sq mi (10,360 km²)
Currency: 100 piastres = 1 pound (Lebanese)
Languages: Arabic, French, English
Religions: Islam, Christianity
Economy: agriculture, fruit, cotton, textiles, tobacco, banking

The cedar tree has been a Lebanese symbol since Biblical times; its use on a white flag appears to date from the 18th century, when the Maronite Christians of Lebanon adopted the symbol, and certainly it appeared on a flag of 1861. When the country came under French mandate in 1920 the flag used was the French tricolour with the cedar tree in the central stripe. In 1943, a few weeks before Lebanon became independent on 1 January 1944, the current version was adopted as the national flag.

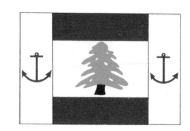

Lebanon's flag at sea

LESOTHO

Kingdom of

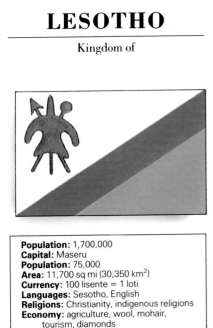

Population: 1,700,000
Capital: Maseru
Population: 75,000
Area: 11,700 sq mi (30,350 km²)
Currency: 100 lisente = 1 loti
Languages: Sesotho, English
Religions: Christianity, indigenous religions
Economy: agriculture, wool, mohair, tourism, diamonds

The current Lesotho flag dates only from 1986, when a coup ousted the ruling Lesotho National Party, whose colours had previously been used for the flag since independence in 1966. The image of the shield with crossed spear and war-club symbolizes the will of the people to defend their nation. The flag also has white for peace, blue for rain and green for prosperity.

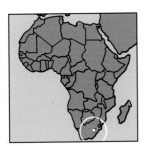

The Royal Standard of Lesotho

LIBERIA

Republic of

Population: 2,500,000
Capital: Monrovia
Population: 307,000
Area: 43,000 sq mi (110,000 km²)
Currency: 100 cents = 1 dollar (Liberian)
Languages: English, indigenous languages
Religions: indigenous religions, Islam, Christianity
Economy: agriculture, rubber, coffee, cocoa, gold, diamonds

The national flag of Liberia, adopted on the country's becoming the first independent Black African republic in 1847, is very obviously modelled on the Stars and Stripes; this is hardly coincidental, since it was largely as a result of the initiatives of a US organization, the American Colonization Society, that freed slaves from the USA were able to return to their ancestral continent and set up in the territory that is now Liberia. A similar flag had been used since 1827, but it had 13 stripes and, in place of the star, a white cross — thereby expressing the relationship with the USA (of which th country was then officially a colony) and the Christian inspiration of the American Colonization Society. The current 11 stripes of the flag denote the 11 signatures on Liberia's Declaration of Independence; the star is for the shining light in darkness that the new country was intended to represent.

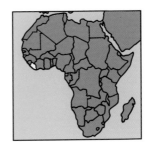

LIBYA

(Popular Socialist Libyan Arab Jamahiriyah)
Al-Jamahiriyah al-Arabiya al-Libya al-Shabiya al-Ishtirakiya

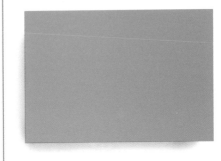

Population: 4,230,000
Capital: Tripoli (Tarabulus)
Population: 990,000
Area: 680,000 sq mi (1,760,000 km²)
Currency: 1000 dirhams = 1 dinar
Language: Arabic
Religion: Islam
Economy: oil, gas, agriculture, textiles, fishing, tobacco

In 1971 Libya adopted the flag of the Federation of Arab Republics, but in 1977, after (possibly government inspired) scenes of rioting and flag-burning in the streets over the decision of Egypt (*q.v.*) one of the federation's other two members, to seek peace with Israel, the current national flag was adopted. This is in plain green to denote the nation's complete devotion to Islam and also the agricultural ("green") revolution dictated by the Libyan leader since a military coup and the abolition of the monarchy in 1969, Moammar al-Gadafi (or Gaddafi; 1942–   ).

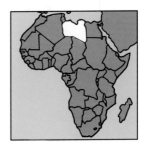

L

LIECHTENSTEIN
Principality of
Fürstentum Liechtenstein

Population: 28,500
Capital: Vaduz
Population: 5,000
Area: 62 sq mi (160 km²)
Currency: 100 centimes = 1 franc (Swiss)
Languages: German, Alemannic
Religion: Christianity (mainly RC)
Economy: banking, tourism, postage stamps

The red and blue of the Liechtenstein flag date back to the early 19th century, and in 1921 the principality adopted them in a straightforward bicolour. One of the less significant political upheavals consequent upon the 1936 Olympic Games in Berlin – "Hitler's Games" – was a result of the discovery that Haiti (*q.v.*) and Leichtenstein had extremely similar flags. Liechtenstein therefore added in 1937 the yellow coronet both to avoid confusion and to indicate the country's status as a principality.

The arms of Liechtenstein

LITHUANIA
Lietuva/Litva

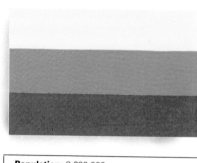

Population: 3,690,000
Capital: Vilnius
Population: 535,000
Area: 25,200 sq mi (65,200 km²)
Languages: Lithuanian, Russian, Lettish
Religion: Roman Catholicism
Economy: rye, sugarbeet, flax, barley, milk, potatoes, meat, shipbuilding, heavy machinery, building materials, textiles, paper, lumber

Lithuania has been a unitary state since 1991, having become so at the time of the general dissolution of the Union of Soviet Socialist Republics. The region, then including much of what is today Ukraine (*q.v.*) was settled by the Lithuanian people before the 12th century, eventually becoming part of the Polish-Lithuanian Empire, which was progressively depleted by the assaults of Germany, Sweden and Russia; by the end of the 18th century almost all of what is now Lithuania was a province of the latter. From 1918 until 1940 Lithuania was independent, its regime being as near fascist as makes no difference; then it was occupied by Russia, followed by Germany in 1941–4. Its annexation by the USSR in 1944 was regarded by a few Western governments, notably that of the USA, as an illegal occupation, so that they continued to recognize Lithuania as an independent nation in the teeth of the reality.

LUXEMBOURG
Grand Duchy of
Grand-Duché de Luxembourg/ Grousherzogdem Lezebuurg

Population: 377,500
Capital: Luxembourg
Population: 79,000
Area: 1,000 sq mi (2,600 km²)
Currency: 100 centimes = 1 franc (Luxembourg & Belgian)
Languages: Letzeburghish, French, German, English
Religion: Christianity (mainly RC)
Economy: financial services, metals, wine, chemicals, agriculture

The flag of Luxembourg is hard to distinguish from that of The Netherlands (*q.v.*); this is partly a consequence of the fact that from 1815 to 1890 Luxembourg was, against its wishes, tagged on to the larger country. In fact, the Luxembourgian use of the colours dates back long before that – to the 13th century, and possibly earlier. From 1845 to 1890 the two flags were identical, but on its release from Netherlands rule Luxembourg, while keeping the same basic flag, opted to use a much paler shade of blue and a more elongated shape.

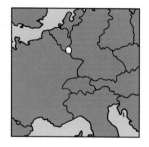

MACAO
See Portugal

MADAGASCAR

Democratic Republic of
République démocratique de Madagascar/
Repoblika demokratika Malagasy

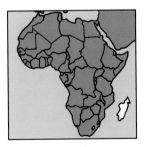

Population: 11,250,000
Capital: Antananarivo (Tananarive)
Population: 800,000
Area: 226,600 sq mi (587,000 km^2)
Currency: 100 centimes = 1 franc
    (Madagascar)
Languages: Malagasy, French
Religions: indigenous religions, Christianity
Economy: coffee, agriculture, vanilla,
    metals

Madagascar became a French protectorate in 1896; it gained autonomy within the French Community in 1958, when it took the name of the Malagasy Republic (which it retained until 1975) and adopted its current flag. Much of the ancestry of the people derives less from Africa than from southeast Asia — and two of the colours of the flag may likewise owe their origins to the more distant continent. These are red and white, the traditional colours used in the flags of the Merina (Hova) people of Madagascar's central plateau, the largest single tribal group, and ruled the country until the French conquest. The green is for the coastal people, the Betsimisaraka, who have ruled since independence.

MADEIRA
See Portugal

MALAWI

Republic of

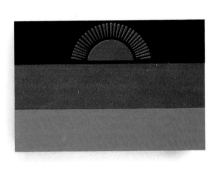

Population: 7,750,000
Capital: Lilongwe
Population: 103,000
Area: 45,750 sq mi (118,500 km^2)
Currency: 100 tambala = 1 kwacha
Languages: Chichewa, English
Religions: Christianity, indigenous
    religions, Islam
Economy: agriculture, tobacco, sugar, tea,
    peanuts, textiles, tourism

The Malawi national flag, adopted on the country's attainment of independence from the UK in 1964, was based on the tricolour adopted in 1953 by the principal political party involved in the struggle for the freedom of the then Nyasaland, the Malawi Congress Party, which took power when its aim was realized; in 1966 Malawi became a one-party republic with Hastings Banda (1905–   ) as president (declared president for life in 1971). The sole revision when the tricolour was adopted as the national flag was the introduction in the black band of a red dawning sun to symbolize the new era. The colours are those of the Black Liberation Movement.

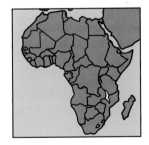

MALAYSIA

Federation of
Persekutuan Tanah Malaysia

M

Population: 17,000,000
Capital: Kuala Lumpur
Population: 938,000
Area: 127,500 sq mi (330,000 km^2)
Currency: 100 sens = 1 ringgit
Languages: Malay, Chinese, Tamil, English,
    indigenous languages
Religions: Islam, Buddhism (Hindu and
    Christian minorities)
Economy: oil, gas, agriculture, metals,
    fishing, electronics, rubber, palm oil,
    pepper, cocoa, pineapples

The Federation of Malaysia, formed in 1963, originally consisted of the 11 states of the previous Federation of Malaya plus Singapore (*q.v.*) and the northern Borneo states of Sarawak and Sabah. The original Malayan flag adopted in 1950 had been inspired in large part by the Stars and Stripes; it had 11 stripes, and the large yellow star had 11 points, in each case as a recognition of the 11 states. When the Federation of Malaysia was formed, the number of both stripes and points was simply increased to 14, and that number was retained even after Singapore's secession in 1965, the "extra" stripe and point now being taken to represent the nation's capital territory, Kuala Lumpur. The star and crescent are Islamic symbols, the red and white are traditional colours, the yellow represents those of the states that are sultanates, and the blue is an acknowledgement of the long history of the British in Malaya.

MALDIVES

Republic of
Divehi Jumhuriya

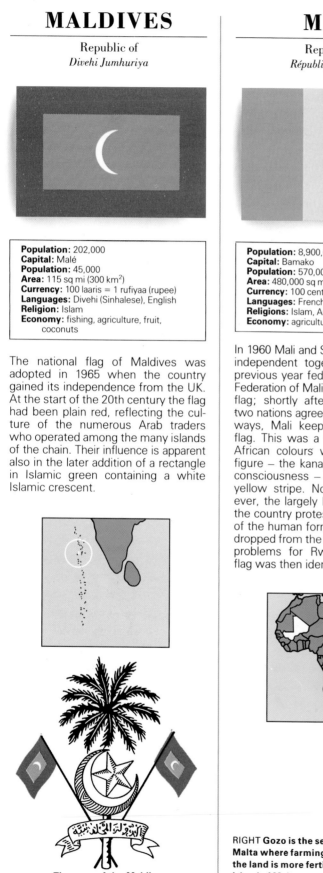

Population: 202,000
Capital: Malé
Population: 45,000
Area: 115 sq mi (300 km²)
Currency: 100 laaris = 1 rufiyaa (rupee)
Languages: Divehi (Sinhalese), English
Religion: Islam
Economy: fishing, agriculture, fruit,
    coconuts

The national flag of Maldives was adopted in 1965 when the country gained its independence from the UK. At the start of the 20th century the flag had been plain red, reflecting the culture of the numerous Arab traders who operated among the many islands of the chain. Their influence is apparent also in the later addition of a rectangle in Islamic green containing a white Islamic crescent.

The arms of the Maldives

MALI

Republic of
République du Mali

Population: 8,900,000
Capital: Bamako
Population: 570,000
Area: 480,000 sq mi (1,240,000 km²)
Currency: 100 centimes = 1 franc (CFA)
Languages: French, indigenous languages
Religions: Islam, Animism
Economy: agriculture, cotton, peanuts

In 1960 Mali and Senegal (*q.v.*) became independent together, having in the previous year federated – to form the Federation of Mali – and adopted a joint flag; shortly after independence the two nations agreed to go their separate ways, Mali keeping both name and flag. This was a tricolour in the Pan-African colours with a black human figure – the kanaga, expressing black consciousness – limned in the central yellow stripe. Not surprisingly, however, the largely Islamic population of the country protested at this depiction of the human form, and in 1961 it was dropped from the flag, thereby causing problems for Rwanda (*q.v.*), whose flag was then identical with Mali's.

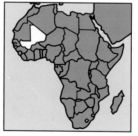

RIGHT **Gozo is the second largest island in Malta where farming is important because the land is more fertile than the larger island of Malta.**

MALTA

Republic of
Republika Ta Malta

Population: 345,600
Capital: Valletta
Population: 14,100
Area: 122 sq mi (315 km²)
Currency: 100 cents = 1 lira (Maltese)
Languages: Maltese, English
Religion: Christianity (almost exclusively
    RC)
Economy: agriculture, shipbuilding and
    repairs, tourism, textiles, electronics

The national flag of Malta dates from 1964 when the island gained its independence from the UK. The red and white coloration dates back much further, having its origins in the various flags used in Malta showing, on a red

background, a white Cross of the Order of the Knights of St John (the "Maltese Cross"), the organization that had ruled the island from 1530 until Malta was conquered by Napoleon in 1798. After Malta was ceded to the UK in 1814 the flag became as the current one, but without the emblem at top left. In 1942 George VI of the UK (1895–1952) awarded the George Cross to the population of Malta as a whole for the courage they had shown during the German and Italian bombardment of the island, and this was commemorated by the addition to the flag of the cross on a square blue background; at the centre of the cross is a medallion showing the saint and the motto "For Gallantry". On independence the blue square was replaced by a thin red border.

MARSHALL ISLANDS

Republic of the

Population: 40,100
Capital: Majuro
Population: 8,700
Area: 70 sq mi (180 km^2)
Currency: 100 cents = 1 dollar (US)
Languages: Marshallese, English
Religion: Christianity
Economy: US aid, agriculture, copra, fishing, coconuts

The Marshall Islands were a German protectorate from 1899, were captured and occupied by Japan during World War I, were taken by the USA during World War II, were administered by the USA as part of the UN Trust Territory of the Pacific from 1947, became self-governing in 1979 and finally became an independent republic in free association with the USA in 1986, an association that may surprise, since the US tested 64 nuclear bombs at Bikina and Enewetak in the Marshalls between 1946 and 1958, and the adverse effects on the local population are still apparent. The current flag dates from 1979. The blue is for the Pacific Ocean, the orange-red for courage and prosperity, and the white for brightness. The four larger rays of the star are for Majuro (the capital) and the three administrative districts; the 20 shorter ones are for the nation's municipalities.

MARTINIQUE
See France

MAURITANIA

Islamic Republic of
République Islamique de Mauritanie

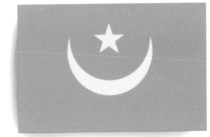

Population: 1,900,000
Capital: Nouakchott
Population: 150,000
Area: 400,000 sq mi (1,031,000 km^2)
Currency: 5 khoums = 1 ouguiya
Languages: Arabic, French, indigenous languages
Religion: Islam
Economy: agriculture, fishing, iron

The Islamic allegiances of Mauritania can hardly be in doubt: the green of her flag as well as the symbol, in yellow, of the crescent with five-pointed star tell the whole story. Mauritania, originally part of French West Africa, gained autonomy within the French Community in 1958 and adopted this flag in 1959, remaining loyal to it on attaining full independence in 1960.

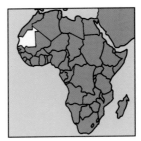

M

MAURITIUS

State of

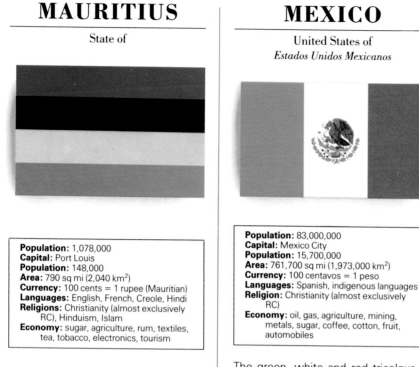

Population: 1,078,000
Capital: Port Louis
Population: 148,000
Area: 790 sq mi (2,040 km²)
Currency: 100 cents = 1 rupee (Mauritian)
Languages: English, French, Creole, Hindi
Religions: Christianity (almost exclusively RC), Hinduism, Islam
Economy: sugar, agriculture, rum, textiles, tea, tobacco, electronics, tourism

The current flag of Mauritius was adopted in 1968 at the time the nation attained its independence. Its colours – red, blue, yellow and green – are those of the coat of arms adopted in 1906. Meanings have been ascribed to the colours since 1968: the red is for the liberation struggle and for the blood spilled in the course of this struggle, the blue is for the Indian Ocean, the yellow is for the sunlight of freedom and for the bright future, and the green is for agriculture and for the all-year-round vegetation of the country.

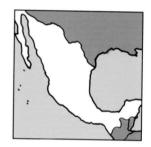

MEXICO

United States of
Estados Unidos Mexicanos

Population: 83,000,000
Capital: Mexico City
Population: 15,700,000
Area: 761,700 sq mi (1,973,000 km²)
Currency: 100 centavos = 1 peso
Languages: Spanish, indigenous languages
Religion: Christianity (almost exclusively RC)
Economy: oil, gas, agriculture, mining, metals, sugar, coffee, cotton, fruit, automobiles

The green, white and red tricolour of Mexico was introduced in 1821, around the time that the country gained its independence; a couple of years later, in 1823, the flag was established with the same basic pattern as it has today, with the three stripes arranged vertically in the present configuration and with the country's arms as an emblem in the centre of the white stripe. The arms themselves have undergone many changes since 1823 (the most recent version is that of 1968), but their scheme has always been that of an eagle eating a snake while perched atop a cactus on an island in a lake. This symbol dates back to the Aztecs, whose legend of the founding of their nation was that their nomadic ancestors were told that they should establish themselves at a place where they came across such a scene; this they did around 1325, founding the city of Tenochtitlán on the site of what is now Mexico City; by the time Hernando Cortés (1485–1547) razed Tenochtitlán in 1521 it had a population of about 500,000, making it a truly vast city for the era.

ABOVE **A colourful mural by Diego Riviera showing the ancient Aztec city of Tenochtitlán (now Mexico City), believed to be the founding city of Mexico.**

MICRONESIA

Federated States of

Population: 86,000
Capital: Kolonia
Population: 5,500
Area: 280 sq mi (720 km²)
Currency: 100 cents = 1 dollar (US)
Languages: English, indigenous languages
Religion: Christianity (mainly RC)
Economy: copra, agriculture, fishing

A federated state in free association with the USA, Micronesia was earlier part of the UN Trust Territory of the Pacific Islands, administered by the USA; she gained her present status in 1985. The first flag for Micronesia was introduced in 1962: it was in the UN colours of pale blue and white, and showed six stars representing the six states that were then a part of the federation. In 1978 the current form of the flag, with four stars to show that there were now only four states, was introduced, and it has remained in use since. Of these four states – Kosrae, Pohnpei, Truk and Yap – Pohnpei, on which stands the capital, Kolonia, accounts for more than 50 per cent of the land area.

MIDWAY ISLAND
See United States of America

MOLDOVA

Moldau, Moldava

Population: 4,341,000
Capital: Kishinev (Kisin'ov)
Population: 605,000
Area: 13,000 sq mi (33,700 km²)
Languages: Russian, Romanian
Religion: Christianity
Economy: grapes, fruit, walnuts, honey, wheat, maize, sugarbeet, sunflowers, tobacco, distilling, food processing, engineering, wine

Moldova has been a unitary state since 1991, having become so at the time of the general dissolution of the Union of Soviet Socialist Republics. The historical region of Moldova is today divided by the Prut River, so that part of it lies in Romania. Between the Prut and the Dniester lies that part of Moldova called Bessarabia; this was ceded to Russia in 1812, became part of Moldova in 1856 after the Crimean War, was regained by Russia in 1878, was controlled almost continuously 1918–44 by Romania and then finally became a part of the Moldovian and Ukrainian SSRs.

MONACO

Principality of
Principauté de Monaco

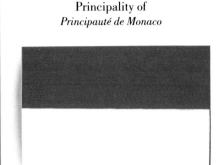

M

Population: 28,000
Capital: Monaco-Ville
Population: 1,650
Area: 0.76 sq mi (1.95 km²)
Currency: 100 centimes = 1 franc (Monégasque and French)
Languages: French, Monégasque
Religion: Christianity (mainly RC)
Economy: gaming, tourism, banking

Except for the proportions, the flag of Monaco is identical with that of Indonesia – a fact about which Monaco has complained on numerous occasions since 1945, when the current Indonesian flag was introduced (officially confirmed 1949). And with some justice, for Monaco's claim is of considerably greater antiquity. Although the flag itself was adopted in its current form only as "recently" as 1881, its colours date back to the 14th century, when they were established by the House of Grimaldi, which has ruled the tiny country since 1297.

The arms of Monaco

MONGOLIA

Mongolian People's Republic
Buğd Nayramdakh Mongol Ard Uls

Population: 2,100,000
Capital: Ulan Bator (Ulaanbaatar)
Population: 435,000
Area: 610,000 sq mi (1,566,500 km²)
Currency: 100 mongo = 1 togrog (tugrik)
Languages: Mongolian, Kazakh
Religions: Shamanism, Buddhism, Islam;
atheism predominant
Economy: agriculture, minerals, meat,
wool, hides, skins, mining

Mongolia was one of the very first communist states, abolishing its monarchy and declaring itself as a people's republic as early as 1924. In 1946 Mongolia's independence was guaranteed by the Sino-Soviet treaty. The current flag dates from a few years earlier, 1940, and combines the archetypal socialist red with blue to symbolize the sky and thereby the Mongol people; beneath the yellow star of socialism at left is an ideogram called the *syonbo*. This includes a traditional Buddhist yin-yang symbol as well as numerous other elements, whose complicated individual interpretation yields a cluster of concepts including that of the five elements (earth, air, fire, water, the aether), death to enemies, the value of friendship and others.

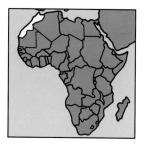

MONTSERRAT
See United Kingdom

MOROCCO

Kingdom of
al-Mamiaka al-Maghrebia

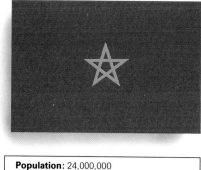

Population: 24,000,000
Capital: Rabat
Population: 840,000
Area: 177,000 sq mi (459,000 km²)
Currency: 100 centimes = 1 dirham
Languages: Arabic, Berber, French,
Spanish
Religion: Islam
Economy: agriculture, fruit, vegetables,
minerals, fishing, fertilizers, wine

Before 1915 Morocco, like many other Arab countries, flew a plain red flag; the green five-pointed star was added, presumably at the urging of the French, in order to obviate confusion. Initially the flag was for use only on land; it became the true national flag only in 1956, when Morocco regained the independence she had lost in 1912, becoming first a sultanate and then almost at once (1957) a kingdom. This particular pentagram is often called the Seal of Solomon or Solomon's Seal; this term should, in fact, be applied only to a rather similar-looking hexagram, best known outside the field of magic as the Star of David, as depicted on the flag of Israel (*q.v.*).

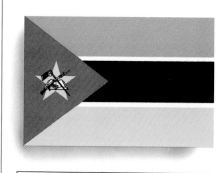

MOZAMBIQUE

People's Republic of
República Popular de Moçambique

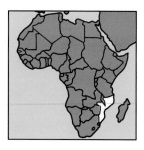

Population: 14,931,000
Capital: Maputo
Population: 786,000
Area: 303,000 sq mi (785,000 km²)
Currency: 100 centavos = 1 metical
Languages: Portuguese, indigenous
languages
Religions: Animism, Christianity, Islam
Economy: agriculture, cashew nuts, tea,
textiles, cotton, mining

The flag adopted by Mozambique on gaining its independence from Portugal in 1975 had the same colours as that of the main party that had spearheaded the fight for liberation, the Frente de Libertaçao de Moçambique (FRELIMO), but a very different design. In 1983 the current design was adopted; it resembles much more closely the previous FRELIMO flag, the party itself having now adopted a different design for its own use. The symbols in the red triangle – five-pointed star, open book, hoe and Kalashnikov rifle – are drawn from the country's coat of arms. The yellow star expresses internationalism, the book education, the hoe agriculture and the Kalashnikov the struggle to attain and if necessary to retain independence. Agriculture and the independence struggle are symbolized also by the use of green and red, respectively, while white is for peace, yellow for the nation's mineral resources and black for the people.

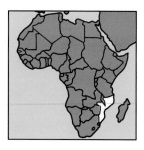

MYANMAR

Socialist Republic of the Union of
Pyidaungsu Myanma Naingngandaw

Population: 40,000,000
Capital: Rangoon (Yangon)
Population: 2,460,000
Area: 261,000 sq mi (676,500 km^2)
Currency: 100 pyas = 1 kyat
Language: Burmese
Religion: Buddhism
Economy: rice, sugar, jute, wood, rubber, oil, gas, metals, mining, fishing

Until 1991 Myanmar was known as Burma. In 1948 it gained its independence from the UK and, rather unusually, left the Commonwealth at the same time, setting up as a democratic republic. In 1962 a military coup led by General U Ne Win (1911–) overthrew democracy, and in 1974 a one-party socialist republic was set up with Ne Win as its president. San Yu (1919–) took over as president in 1981, and since 1988 the country's president has been General Saw Maung, despite the fact that the opposition National League for Democracy, led by the charismatic winner of the 1991 Nobel Peace Prize, Daw Aung San Suu Kyi (1945–), herself under house arrest since 1989, won a landslide victory in elections held in 1990. The present design of the flag dates from the new constitution of 1974, differing from the 1948 flag only in regard to the emblem on the blue rectangle. This now shows a rice plant set in front of a 14-toothed cogwheel, which is surrounded by a ring of stars, one per tooth; this reflects the fact that Myanmar is made up of seven states and seven provinces.

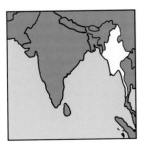

NAMIBIA

Population: 1,750,000
Capital: Windhoek
Population: 89,000
Area: 318,300 sq mi (824,300 km^2)
Currency: 100 cents = 1 rand (South African)
Languages: English, Afrikaans, German, Bantu
Religions: Christianity, indigenous languages
Economy: diamonds, metals, agriculture, livestock, fishing .

Until March 1990 Namibia was a territory technically described as "unlawfully occupied" by South Africa – i.e., its government was enforcedly a puppet of the apartheid state. The resistance to the illegal rule had been led by the South-West Africa People's Organization (SWAPO), and it had been widely expected that the SWAPO flag – a straightforward tricolour of blue, red and green in horizontal bands – would be adopted as the national flag. Instead, however, although the colours were indeed adopted, they were used in a quite different arrangement, and a prominent sun was added to symbolize both the climate and the bright light of a nation at last released from servitude.

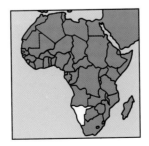

NAURU

Republic of
Naoero

Population: 9,000
Centre of government: Yaren
Population: 430
Area: 8 sq mi (21 km^2)
Currency: 100 cents = 1 dollar (Australian)
Languages: Nauruan, English
Religion: Christianity (mainly Protestant)
Economy: phosphates

The flag of Nauru was introduced in 1968 when the country attained her independence, having previously been, since 1947, under the joint trusteeship of Australia, New Zealand and the UK; independent Nauru was admitted to the Commonwealth as a special member. The winner of a design competition, the flag has a 12-pointed star symbolizing Nauru herself, lying in the blue Pacific Ocean one degree south of the yellow Equator. The points of the star are for the 12 original tribes of the island.

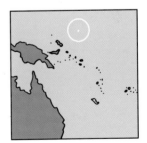

The arms of Nauru

N

NEPAL

Kingdom of
Sri Nepala Sarkar

Population: 18,250,000
Capital: Katmandu (Kathmandu)
Population: 394,000
Area: 54,360 sq mi (140,790 km²)
Currency: 100 paisa = 1 rupee (Nepalese)
Languages: Nepali, other indigenous
    languages
Religion: Hinduism (Buddhist and Islamic
    minorities)
Economy: rice, agriculture, jute, wood,
    sugar, leather

The most striking feature of the Nepalese flag on first sight is its shape: it is the only national flag not to be rectangular. The origin of this shape is fairly obvious: before the late 19th century two pennants were flown together; these were then joined to make a single entity. The two symbols represent the moon (upper) and sun. Until 1951 and their downfall, the sun represented the Ráná family, which had held prime ministerial office and effective control of the nation, while the moon was for the royal family. The modern form of this centuries-old flag dates only from 1962, when the human faces that had previously adorned both symbols were deleted.

NETHERLANDS

Kingdom of the
Köninkrijk der Nederlanden

Population: 14,760,000
Capital: Amsterdam
Population: 676,500
Seat of government: The Hague (Den
    Haag, La Haie, 's-Gravenhage)
Population: 450,000
Area: 16,050 sq mi (41,550 km²)
Currency: 100 cents = 1 guilder (florin)
Languages: Dutch, Frisian
Religion: Christianity
Economy: oil-refining, shipbuilding, iron,
    steel, textiles, machinery, electrical
    equipment, plastics, dairy produce,
    financial services, tourism,
    transportation

The red, white and blue tricolour of the Netherlands flag originated in the flags used by supporters – notably at sea – of William the Silent (1533–84), Prince of Orange, in his campaigns to expel the Spanish. The *Prinsenvlag*, as it came to be known, was accepted as the sole Dutch flag from 1597; but from about 1630 the orange band was frequently rendered in red, and in 1796, the year after the country had been conquered by the French, the orange was prohibited, so that the flag shared the colours of the French tricolour – whose colours, ironically, it had inspired in the first place! In 1937 the specified shade of blue was changed, but otherwise the flag has remained unaltered.

NETHERLANDS ASSOCIATED LANDS

Aruba

Population: 62,500
Capital: Oranjestad
Population: 16,500
Area: 75 sq mi (195 km²)
Economy: oil processing, tourism

Until 1986, when the two opted to have separate status, Aruba was part of the Netherlands Antilles. Its flag in fact dates from 1976.

Netherlands Antilles

Population: 190,000
Capital: Willemstad
Population: 94,150
Area: 308 sq mi (800 km²)
Economy: oil processing, tourism

Until 1986, when the two opted to have separate status, the Netherlands Antilles included also Aruba, and its flag contained six stars. Today's flag is identical except that it bears only five stars, one for each of the remaining island groups. The colours are those of the Netherlands flag.

NEW CALEDONIA
See France

NEW ZEALAND

Dominion of

N

Population: 3,300,000
Capital: Wellington
Population: 344,000
Area: 103,700 sq mi (268,700 km^2)
Currency: 100 cents = 1 dollar (NZ)
Languages: English, Maori
Religion: Christianity (mainly Protestant)
Economy: meat, dairy products, wool, gas,
    coal, paper, metals, machinery,
    agriculture, fishing, fruit, hides,
    tourism

The flag of New Zealand was designed and introduced for restricted use in 1869 and adopted as the national flag in 1902. It is the British Blue Ensign with a very stylized version of the Southern Cross, showing only four stars; these are red, limned in white. The design has survived New Zealand's becoming a dominion in 1907 and achieving full independence in 1931. A very similar design was introduced in 1870 in Australia (*q.v.*) by the state of Victoria.

NEW ZEALAND — ASSOCIATED LANDS

Cook Islands

Population: 17,750
Centre of government: Avarua
Population: 850
Area: 93 sq mi (240 km^2)
Economy: agriculture, fruit, yams, fishing,
    copra, vegetables, textiles

The current flag of the Cook Islands was adopted in 1979. Like that of New Zealand, it is the British Blue Ensign. The 15 stars represent the 15 main islands of the group; they are arranged in a circle to indicate that no one island is more important than any of the others. Unlike the stars of the New Zealand flag, these are simply in white as an expression of peace.

The flag of the Queen of New Zealand

Niue Island

Population: 2,300
Administrative centre: Alofi
Area: 100 sq mi (260 km^2)
Economy: coconuts, copra, fruit

The Niue flag, adopted in 1974, could be described as an adaptation of the British Yellow Ensign, if there were such a thing! The yellow background is claimed to represent both sunshine and the warmth of the people's feelings towards the Commonwealth, especially towards New Zealand. The connection with the UK is stressed by the use of the Union Jack, that with New Zealand by the four small stars on the St George's Cross, which echo the appearance of the Southern Cross on the New Zealand flag. The large star at the centre of the cross is Niue itself; it is set on a blue disc to convey the idea of Niue as a remote island.

Tokelau

Population: 1,800
Administrative centre: Atafu
Area: 4.6 sq mi (12 km^2)
Economy: coconuts, copra

This territory uses the New Zealand flag.

**Mount Egmont on North Island,
New Zealand last erupted 300 years ago.**

NICARAGUA

Republic of
República de Nicaragua

Population: 3,620,000
Capital: Managua
Population: 630,000
Area: 50,200 sq mi (130,000 km²)
Currency: 100 centavos = 1 córdoba
Language: Spanish
Religion: Christianity (almost exclusively RC)
Economy: cotton, coffee, agriculture, gold, silver, copper, fishing

Until 1821 Nicaragua was part of the captaincy-general of Guatemala, which was ruled by Spain; in that year the captaincy-general as a whole declared independence but was almost immediately swallowed up by the Mexican Empire. By 1824 Nicaragua and most of the other relevant provinces – notably Costa Rica, El Salvador, Guatemala and Honduras – had regained their freedom and formed the Central American Federation (or United Provinces of Central America), a loosely knit arrangement that was soon to be unravelled, in 1838. The flag of the CAF was a simple blue and white tri-band, and it was to this design that Nicaragua turned in 1908. The flag may be used plain or with the national arms, which show, in a triangular frame, volcanoes, a rainbow (peace) and the Cap of Liberty. Compare the arms of El Salvador (*q.v.*).

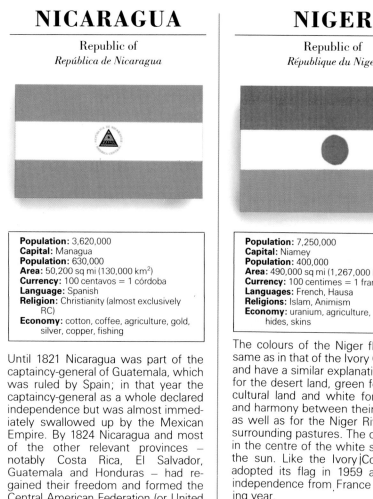

NIGER

Republic of
République du Niger

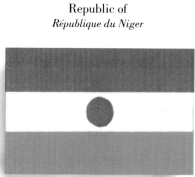

Population: 7,250,000
Capital: Niamey
Population: 400,000
Area: 490,000 sq mi (1,267,000 km²)
Currency: 100 centimes = 1 franc (CFA)
Languages: French, Hausa
Religions: Islam, Animism
Economy: uranium, agriculture, peanuts, hides, skins

The colours of the Niger flag are the same as in that of the Ivory Coast (*q.v.*) and have a similar explanation: orange for the desert land, green for the agricultural land and white for the unity and harmony between their peoples – as well as for the Niger River and its surrounding pastures. The orange disc in the centre of the white stripe is for the sun. Like the Ivory Coast, Niger adopted its flag in 1959 and gained independence from France the following year.

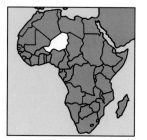

NIGERIA

Federation of

Population: 105,000,000
Capital: Lagos
Population: 1,400,000
Area: 357,000 sq mi (924,000 km²)
Currency: 100 kobo = 1 naira
Languages: English, Yoruba, Hausa, Ibo
Religions: Islam, Christianity, indigenous religions
Economy: oil, gas, agriculture, mining, tin, iron, coal, cocoa, wood, hides

The Nigerian flag, which was adopted in 1960 when the country attained its independence from the UK, was adapted from the winning design of a public competition. The green reflects the importance to the country of its forests and agriculture, while the white represents the desire for peace and unity – a sad irony in light of the brutal civil war that racked the country between 1967 and 1970, when the Ibo people of Biafra (Iboland), Nigeria's eastern region, unilaterally declared independence. The war and the concomitant famine cost about a million lives and aroused world sympathy for the Ibo plight. For the three short years of its existence Biafra had a flag somewhat similar to that of Malawi (*q.v.*), but with the black and red stripes swapped and the rising sun on the black stripe being in gold rather than red.

NIEU ISLAND
See New Zealand

NORFOLK ISLAND
See Australia

NORTHERN MARIANA ISLANDS

Commonwealth of the

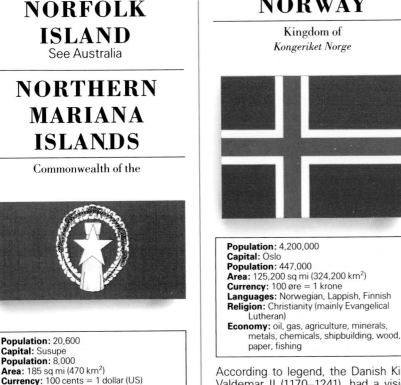

Population: 20,600
Capital: Susupe
Population: 8,000
Area: 185 sq mi (470 km²)
Currency: 100 cents = 1 dollar (US)
Languages: English, Carolinian, Chamorro
Religion: Christianity (mainly RC)
Economy: tourism, coconuts, fishing, fruit, vegetables

When the UN Trust Territory of the Pacific Islands, which was administered by the USA, was falling apart during the 1970s, only the Northern Marianas opted to retain close ties with the USA rather than to become fully independent immediately; in 1976 the country's status therefore officially became that of a commonwealth in association with the USA. The blue background of the flag, created in 1972, represents the Pacific Ocean or the United Nations (*q.v.*), whose blue it is, and the star expresses the commonwealth; the grey shape represents a latte or taga stone, an artefact representative of the Chamorro ancestors of the majority of the islands' population.

NORWAY

Kingdom of
Kongeriket Norge

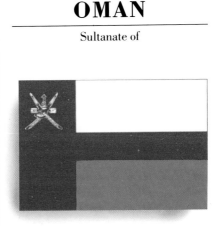

Population: 4,200,000
Capital: Oslo
Population: 447,000
Area: 125,200 sq mi (324,200 km²)
Currency: 100 øre = 1 krone
Languages: Norwegian, Lappish, Finnish
Religion: Christianity (mainly Evangelical Lutheran)
Economy: oil, gas, agriculture, minerals, metals, chemicals, shipbuilding, wood, paper, fishing

According to legend, the Danish King Valdemar II (1170–1241), had a vision on the eve of the Battle of Lyndanisse of a white crucifix in the darkening sky; this he interpreted to mean that Christ wished him to triumph in slaughter on the morrow, which he duly did. Thus was born the Scandinavian Cross, seen also in the flags of Finland, Iceland (*qq.v.*), Norway and Sweden (*q.v.*), the cross was originally square, but over the centuries one of its horizontals was extended. The Norwegian version dates from 1821, when Norway was still a part of Sweden, having been ceded by Denmark seven years before. The flag was essentially the Danish one but with the addition of a blue cross superimposed on the white, so that the colour scheme expressed Norwegian nationalism by echoing the French tricolour; it was for use only in coastal waters. In 1898, a few years before the gaining of full independence in 1905, Norway was at last able to use the design as her national flag.

OMAN

Sultanate of

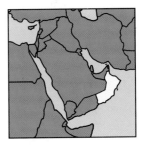

Population: 1,375,000
Capital: Muscat (Masqat)
Population: 30,000
Area: 82,000 sq mi (212,500 km²)
Currency: 1000 baiza = 1 rial (Omani)
Languages: Arabic, English
Religion: Islam
Economy: oil, agriculture, fruit, copper, fishing

The current flag of Oman was introduced in 1970 (and slightly revised in 1987), replacing the traditional plain red flag. The emblem now used is likewise traditional; it shows a curved dagger fastened over a pair of crossed sabres. The red has retained its customary Islamic significance; the white band is, of course, for peace but also expresses the authority of the imam, while the green band is for Islam and for the Jabel Akhdhar (or Green Mountain range), which lies towards the north of the country.

O

The emblem of Oman

PAKISTAN

Islamic Republic of
Islami Jumhouryat-e-Pakistan

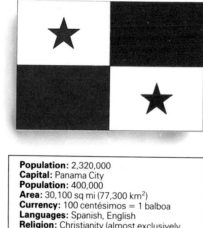

Population: 105,000,000
Capital: Islamabad
Population: 205,000
Area: 310,400 sq mi (804,000 km²)
Currency: 100 paisas = 1 rupee (Pakistani)
Languages: Urdu, English, Punjabi, Sindhi, Pushtu, Baluchi, Bravi
Religion: Islam (Hindu and Christian minorities)
Economy: cotton, rice, sugar, tobacco, agriculture, gas, metal, leather, manufactured goods

The All-Indian Muslim League, whose activities were largely responsible for Pakistan gaining her independence in 1947, had in 1906 adopted as its flag the Islamic crescent and star on a background of equally Islamic green (in this case described as "tartan" green). It seemed only just that the League's flag be adopted also as the national flag, but at the last moment before independence it was pointed out that, while the majority of the population was Muslim, there were minorities who adhered to other faiths. The vertical white stripe was therefore added to symbolize tolerance of those faiths.

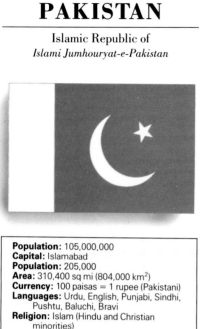

PANAMA

Republic of
República de Panamá

Population: 2,320,000
Capital: Panama City
Population: 400,000
Area: 30,100 sq mi (77,300 km²)
Currency: 100 centésimos = 1 balboa
Languages: Spanish, English
Religion: Christianity (almost exclusively RC)
Economy: petroleum products, tourism, financial services, services related to Panama Canal, drug trafficking, bananas, sugar, shrimps

Panama achieved its independence (in 1903) from Colombia, of which it had been a province, largely thanks to US assistance because the Americans were eager to build a canal through the isthmus and the Colombians would not let them; a narrow strip of land to either side of the canal is still controlled by the USA. Perhaps in gratitude to their US deliverers, the Panamanians adopted the colours red, white and blue for their flag, although an alternative explanation is that these colours represented the two leading political parties of the time, and that the equal prestige given to each expresses the hope that the two should take turns governing the nation. White has its usual meaning, as do the stars, although the colours of the latter, taken in conjunction with their shape, were intended also to express the rule of law (red) and civic virtues (blue). Since 1979 the flag has been adopted for the canal zone as well.

PAPUA NEW GUINEA

State of

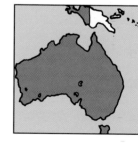

Population: 3,560,000
Capital: Port Moresby
Population: 144,000
Area: 178,000 sq mi (461,700 km²)
Currency: 100 toae = 1 kina
Languages: English, Pidgin English and perhaps 750 localized languages
Religions: Christianity, Animism, indigenous religions
Economy: coffee, cocoa, gold, copper, wood and wood products, agriculture, fishing, palm oil, coconuts, copra, tea, sugar

Designed by the winner of a design competition, the flag of Papua New Guinea was adopted in 1971, four years before the attainment of independence from Australia. The Australian presence lingers on in the use of the five-starred version of the Southern Cross, although here the stars are five-pointed. The yellow bird of paradise not only honours a prominent member of the local fauna but also expresses liberty. The colours were selected purely because they are used frequently in the native art.

66

PARAGUAY

Republic of
República del Paraguay

Population: 4,040,000
Capital: Asunción
Population: 456,000
Area: 157,000 sq mi (407,000 km^2)
Currency: 100 céntimos = 1 guarani
Languages: Spanish, Guarani
Religion: Christianity (almost exclusively RC)
Economy: agriculture, cotton, meat, tobacco, soya, vegetable oil, textiles

After gaining independence in 1811 Paraguay adopted a tricolour as its flag, but the red-white-blue colour combination was not established until the following year. In 1821 the arms were added to the central white band; they show a golden star, the Star of May, to honour the fact that it was on the night of 14 May that independence was declared. From 1842 a different emblem was used for the reverse side of the flag. This was the so-called Treasury Seal, which depicts a lion guarding the cap of liberty and bears the motto *Paz y Justicia* ("Peace with Justice"). Paraguay's is the only national flag whose reverse differs from its obverse.

PERU

Republic of
República del Perú

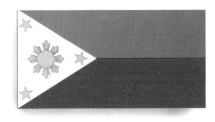

Population: 21,260,000
Capital: Lima
Population: 4,900,000
Area: 496,000 sq mi (1,285,000 km^2)
Currency: 100 centavos = 1 sol
Languages: Spanish, Quechua, Aimara
Religion: Christianity (almost exclusively RC)
Economy: agriculture, oil, mining, metals, cotton, sugar, coffee, textiles, fishing, chemicals, fruit

The colours of the Peruvian flag represent peace and justice (white) and the blood of those who lost their lives in the struggle for independence (red). The colour scheme was initially devised in 1820 by the great liberating General José de San Martín (1778–1850) who, it is claimed, was inspired by the sight of a flock of flamingoes flying over his troops. The design suffered alterations until, in 1825, Simón Bolívar (1783–1830) determined that there should be three vertical stripes arranged in the current fashion.

PHILIPPINES

Republic of the
Republika ng Pilipinas/República de Filipinas

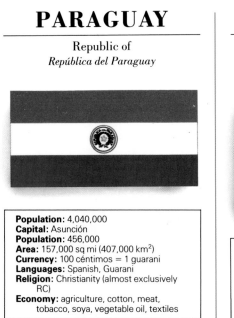

Population: 58,720,000
Capital: Manila
Population: 6,800,000
Area: 115,800 sq mi (300,000 km^2)
Currency: 100 centavos = 1 peso
Languages: Pilipino, English, Spanish
Religion: Christianity (Islamic minority)
Economy: agriculture, electrical goods, fishing, textiles, sugar, fruit, coconuts, chemicals, wood products, rubber, tobacco

The current flag of the Philippnes was adopted in 1946, when the country gained independence from the USA. The flag had first been adopted in 1898, the year that the Philippines declared independence from the Spanish, and was almost immediately (and more or less voluntarily) taken over by the USA. The 1898 flag was used until 1907 and from 1921 until the arrival of the Japanese in 1941. The blue is for idealism, the white for purity and peace, and the red for gallantry and determination. The three small yellow stars signify the two main islands plus the Visayan island group; the large star is the sun and has eight rays to commemorate the eight provinces that first took up the torch of independence in 1896.

PITCAIRN ISLAND

See United Kingdom

P

POLAND

Rzeczpospolita Polska

Population: 37,900,000
Capital: Warsaw (Warszawa)
Population: 1,650,000
Area: 121,900 sq mi (313,000 km^2)
Currency: 100 groszy = 1 zloty
Language: Polish
Religion: Christianity (almost exclusively RC)
Economy: machinery, shipbuilding, agriculture, coal, minerals, automobiles, clothing

The arms of Poland, depicting a white eagle on a red background, date back at least as far as the 13th century, and white and red were adopted as the Polish national colours in 1831. The flag using them, dates from 1919, and since then various revised interpretations have been foisted on to the colours; for example, until the Solidarity movement took over the reins of power in 1989 it was popular to explain the colours as an expression of the people's joint desire for peace and socialism.

PORTUGAL

Republic of
República Portuguesa

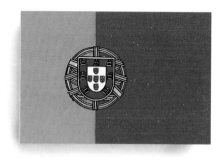

Population: 10,400,000
Capital: Lisbon (Lisboa)
Population: 808,000
Area: 35,800 sq mi (92,000 km^2)
Currency: 100 centavos = 1 escudo
Language: Portuguese
Religion: Christianity (almost exclusively RC)
Economy: agriculture, textiles, machinery, metals, chemicals, cork, wine, sardines

In 1910 the Portuguese monarchy was ousted and a republic established, and it is from this year that the current flag and the prominence on it of revolutionary red both date. The green, often taken to express hope or the sea, can be traced back to the time of Henry the Navigator (1394–1460), who inspired and sponsored a whole generation of Portuguese maritime explorers. The depiction of the armillary sphere at the centre of the flag likewise links with Henry the Navigator, being an emblem chosen to commemorate the deeds of Henry and his protégés by King Manuel I (1469–1521), whose reign saw a further great surge of Portuguese exploration.

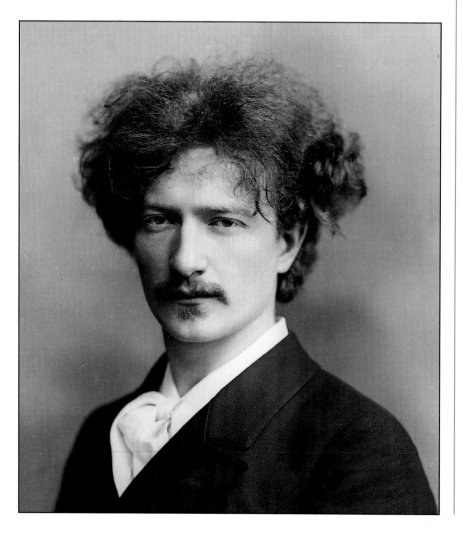

LEFT Ignace Jan Padewerski, Polish patriot and one of the greatest piano virtuosi of the turn of the century, led Polish demands for freedom during the First World War. He became the first president of re-born Poland following Allied victory.

PORTUGAL—ASSOCIATED LANDS

Azores

Açores

Population: 244,000
Capital: Ponta Delgada
Population: 55,000
Area: 870 sq mi (2,250 km²)
Economy: agriculture, fruit, animal husbandry, fishing, whaling

The current flag of the Azores was introduced in 1979, three years after the islands had gained self-government. The Azores were named for the goshawk, and so it is only fitting that a depiction of this bird should be central to the design. The nine stars arced above it represent the nine main islands of the group. In the top left appear the Portuguese state arms.

Macao

Macau: Aomen

Population: 444,000
Capital: Macao City
Population: 277,000
Area: 6 sq mi (15.5 km²)
Economy: textiles, tourism, fishing

The flag used in Macao is that of Portugal.

Madeira

Madeira Islands: Funchal Islands

Population: 254,000
Capital: Funchal
Population: 45,500
Area: 305 sq mi (790 km²)
Economy: wine, tourism, bananas, sugar, basketwork

Introduced in 1978, the flag of Madeira has at its centre the Cross of the Knights of the Order of Christ. The blue and yellow are often interpreted as expressing the ocean and sunshine, respectively, but the traditional meanings of the colours among the islanders are peace and beauty (blue) and faith and prosperity (yellow).

PUERTO RICO

Commonwealth of

Population: 3,600,000
Capital: San Juan
Population: 435,000
Area: 3,450 sq mi (8,900 km²)
Currency: 100 cents = 1 dollar (US)
Languages: Spanish, English
Religion: Christianity (mainly RC)
Economy: oil refining, chemicals, sugar, livestock, clothing, fishing, machinery, tobacco

Puerto Rico became a commonwealth of the USA in 1952, at which time she adopted as her national flag (which may be flown only in conjunction with the US flag) a design that had first been created in 1895 by the Cuban Revolutionary Party's Puerto Rican branch, an important liberation movement in the struggle for independence from Spain. The flag is very similar to that of Cuba (*q.v.*) but with the stripes in blue and the triangle in red, rather than the other way about. In light of the later history of the two countries' relationships with the USA the similarity is ironic.

P

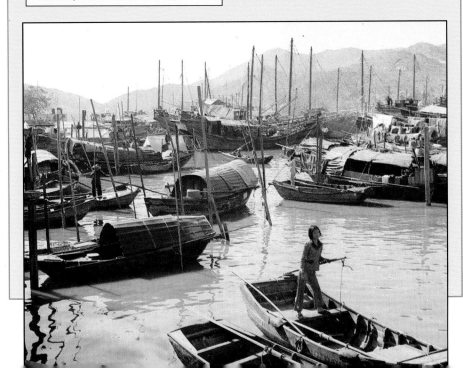

LEFT Macau is a tiny Portuguese territory on the southeast coast of China. The Portuguese first settled there in 1557.

QATAR

State of
Dawlat Qatar

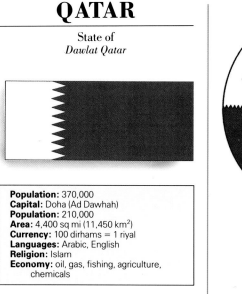

Population: 370,000
Capital: Doha (Ad Dawhah)
Population: 210,000
Area: 4,400 sq mi (11,450 km^2)
Currency: 100 dirhams = 1 riyal
Languages: Arabic, English
Religion: Islam
Economy: oil, gas, fishing, agriculture,
chemicals

Before 1820 a number of the states around the Persian Gulf had the plain red flags of the Kharidjite sect of Islam. Many vessels flying such flags practised piracy on occidental ships, and so in that year the British decreed that in future all such vessels would be assumed to be pirates unless their flags bore white in addition to the red. It was not until the mid-1850s that Qatar complied with this dictum. Her flag was then very similar to that of Bahrain (*q.v.*), but in 1949 the problem was solved by Qatar replacing the red by a curious deep maroon. This may have been a matter of official recognition following long after the fact, since the red vegetable dyes used to colour the flag may well have faded to a shade like this in the heat of the desert sun.

REUNION
See New Zealand

The emblem of Qatar

The state arms of Qatar

ROMANIA

România

Population: 23,050,000
Capital: Bucharest (Bucuresti)
Population: 1,960,000
Area: 92,000 sq mi (237,500 km^2)
Currency: 100 bani = 1 leu
Language: Romanian
Religion: Christianity (mainly Romanian
Orthodox)
Economy: machinery, agriculture, oil,
mining, wood products, shipbuilding,
metals, coal, automobiles, textiles

Until the downfall of the repressive communist regime of Nicolae Ceauşescu (1918–89) in 1989 the Romanian flag bore communist arms in its central yellow stripe. Before 1859 the land that is now Romania consisted of two separate principalities, Wallachia and Moldavia. The Wallachian colours were blue and yellow; those of Moldavia were blue and red. When the two were united it was simple to devise a flag representing all three of the relevant colours, and this was done as early as 1848, when nationalist rumblings were beginning to stir the land. The flag was accepted in 1859 when the two principalities united (two years later they jointly took the name Romania), and in 1866 a rearrangement to make the flag resemble the French tricolour was adopted; this is the form in use today. At the time of writing it is not known if Romania will opt once more to have a coat of arms in the central stripe.

RUSSIAN FEDERATION

Population: 143,078,000
Capital: Moscow (Moskva)
Population: 8,642,000
Area: 6,592,800 sq mi (17,075,400 km²)
Currency: 100 kopeks = 1 rouble
Languages: Russian and numerous others
Religions: Christianity, Islam (Jewish minority)
Economy: engineering, oil, gas, agriculture, fishing, minerals, metals, coal, textiles, electronics, chemicals, animal husbandry, fruit, vegetables, transportation equipment, clothing, automobiles, fertilizers, shipbuilding

The Russian Federation is a loosely knit collection of republics including much of what was until 1991 the Union of Soviet Socialist Republics; many of the other SSRs have become unitary states and now have equal ranking with it in the Commonwealth of Independent States, of which it is the largest member (see entries on Armenia, Azerbaijan, Belorussia, Estonia, Georgia, Kazakhstan, Kirgizstan, Latvia, Lithuania, Moldova, Tajikistan, Turkmenia, Uzbekistan and Ukraine). At the time of writing (March 1992), there are 17 autonomous republics within the Federation, and the details of these are given in the table. Before the dissolution of the USSR, the republics which now form the Federation were responsible for about one-half of Soviet agricultural output and over 60 per cent of Soviet industrial production. Clearly it would be unwise to make over-dogmatic predictions about even the near future of the Russian Federation and of the Commonwealth of Independent States.

RWANDA

Republic of
République rwandaise

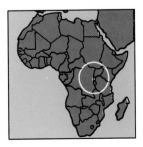

R

Population: 6,755,000
Capital: Kigali
Population: 160,000
Area: 10,200 sq mi (26,300 km²)
Currency: 100 centimes = 1 franc (Rwandan)
Languages: Kinyarwanda, French, Kiswahili
Religions: Christianity, indigenous religions, Islam
Economy: agriculture, coffee, tea, pyrethrum, tin, tungsten, hides

In January 1961 the Hutu people of the northern part of the Belgian-administrated UN Trust Territory of Ruanda-Urundi – the southern part is now Burundi (*q.v.*) – overthrew the ruling Tutsi people and declared their country an independent republic; recognized by Belgium in the following year. Since then the country has suffered a depressing cycle of massacres of the Tutsi by the Hutu. The first flag raised in 1961, a tricolour in the Pan-African colours of red, green and yellow, was much like that of Mali (*q.v.*), and the similarity became an identity a few weeks later when Mali modified her flag. The Hutu therefore changed their flag by simply reversing the order of the colours to their present arrangement. Unfortunately, this made the flag identical with that of Guinea, and so a prominent R – standing not only for Rwanda but also for referendum and revolution, the "three Rs" of a popular nationalist slogan – was added to the central stripe to avoid confusion.

AUTONOMOUS REPUBLICS WITHIN THE RUSSIAN FEDERATION

Name	Population	Capital
Bashkir	3,952,000	Ufa
Buryat	985,000	Ulan-Ude
Chechen-Ingush	1,277,000	Grozny
Chuvash	1,336,000	Cheboksary
Dagestan	1,792,000	Makhachkala
Kabardino-Balkar	760,000	Nalchik
Kalmyk	322,000	Elista
Kara-Kalpak	861,000	Nukus
Karelia	792,000	Petrozavodsk
Komi	1,263,000	Syktyvkar
Mari	750,000	Yoskar-Ola
Mordovia	964,000	Saransk
North Ossetia	634,000	Ordzhonikidze
Tatar	3,640,000	Kazan
Tuva	276,000	Kyzyl
Udmurt	1,609,000	Izhevsk
Yakut	965,000	Yakutsk

ST. HELENA & DEPENDENCIES
See United Kingdom

ST KITTS-NEVIS
Federation of
St Christopher-Nevis

Population: 49,000
Capital: Basseterre
Population: 16,000
Area: 100 sq mi (260 km²)
Currency: 100 cents = 1 dollar (East Caribbean)
Language: English
Religion: Christianity (mainly Protestant)
Economy: sugar, agriculture, textiles, electronics, tourism

Independence came to St Kitts-Nevis in 1983, and with it the current flag; until 1980 the country had been, with Anguilla (*q.v.*), part of the associate state of St Kitts-Nevis-Anguilla. The colours are green for fertility, red for the liberation struggle, black for the African heritage and yellow for sunshine; the white stars express hope and freedom.

ST LUCIA

Population: 146,600
Capital: Castries
Population: 47,000
Area: 240 sq mi (620 km²)
Currency: 100 cents = 1 dollar (East Caribbean)
Languages: English, French
Religion: Christianity (mainly RC)
Economy: bananas, cocoa, coconuts, distillation, cardboard

The basic design of the St Lucia flag was established in 1967, when the country became internally self-governing; it was created by a local artist. In 1979 St Lucia attained full independence, and the flag's proportions were amended and the central symbol enlarged. That symbol represents the Pitons, twin conical volcanic plugs that rise sheerly and impressively from the sea at the southwest of the island. The black and white of the major triangle are for the black and white communities and the harmony between them; the yellow triangle is for sandy beaches; and the blue background is for the ocean.

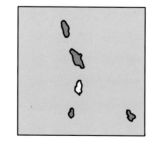

ST. PIERRE ET MIQUELON
See France

ST VINCENT AND THE GRENADINES

Population: 114,000
Capital: Kingstown
Population: 25,000
Area: 150 sq mi (390 km²)
Currency: 100 cents = 1 dollar (East Caribbean)
Languages: English, French
Religion: Christianity (mainly Protestant)
Economy: bananas, agriculture, arrowroot, taro, copra, distillation

St Vincent and the Grenadines became internally self-governing in 1969 and attained full independence in 1979, at which time it adopted the predecessor of its current flag. In 1792 Captain William Bligh (*c*1753–1815), brought to St Vincent from Tahiti some breadfruit trees with which he hoped to provide a food-source for the slaves. The slaves preferred the plentiful indigenous foods, but Bligh's effort is still acknowledged in the nation's flag, albeit unrecognizably. The 1979 flag had, on its central yellow stripe, the national arms supported on a broad breadfruit leaf. In 1985, the arms disappeared, and the leaf was represented in very stylized form by three green diamonds. The yellow stripe was broadened, and the thin white stripes that had separated it from the blue and green were eliminated.

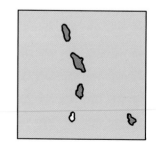

SAMOA
See United States of America and Western Samoa

SAN MARINO

Republic of
Repubblica di San Marino

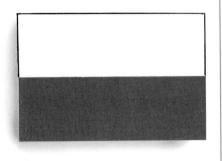

Population: 23,000
Capital: San Marino
Population: 4,500
Area: 24 sq mi (61 km²)
Currency: 100 centesimi = 1 lira (Italian)
Language: Italian
Religion: Christianity (almost exclusively RC)
Economy: tourism, agriculture, wine, postage stamps

San Marino has the curious distinction of being the world's smallest republic. Its flag is known from as far back as 1797. The colours are taken from the arms: the white represents the snow on Monte Titano and the clouds in the sky above it, and the blue signifies the sky itself.

SÃO TOMÉ AND PRÍNCIPE

Democratic Republic of
Republica democratica de São Tomé e Príncipe

Population: 115,000
Capital: São Tomé
Population: 17,000
Area: 372 sq mi (965 km²)
Currency: 100 centavos = 1 dobra
Languages: Portuguese, Creole, indigenous languages
Religions: Christianity, Animism
Economy: agriculture, cocoa, copra, coconuts, wood

The two black stars in the flag, adopted in 1975 on the attainment of independence from Portugal, represent the republic's two islands. The colours are in accordance with the Pan-African colours and have their customary meanings except for the yellow, which is taken to represent the nation's cocoa plantations. The flag is closely based on that adopted three years earlier by the MLSTP (Movement for the Liberation of São Tomé and Príncipe), the sole difference being that the yellow stripe is wider in the national flag.

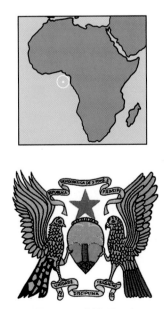

The arms of São Tomé

SAUDI ARABIA

Kingdom of
al-Mamiaka al-'Arabiya as-Sa'udiya

Population: 14,000,000
Capital: Riyadh (Ar-Riyad)
Population: 1,250,000
Area: 830,000 sq mi (2,150,000 km²)
Currency: 100 hallalas = 1 riyal
Languages: Arabic, English
Religion: Islam
Economy: oil, gas, agriculture, chemicals, fertilizers

From about the mid-18th century the Saud family strove to dominate the many warring peoples of the Arabian peninsula, and they took as their flag the green banner believed to have been used by Muhammad himself; by 1932 they had succeeded in subjugating the vast majority of the territory and established the Kingdom of Saudi Arabia. The text in Arabic was added to the flag in 1901; it is a statement analogous to the Christian Creed, and reads: "There is no God but Allah, and Muhammad is Allah's Prophet." The emblem of the sword, incorporated in 1906, refers specifically to Ibn Saud (1880–1953), who, after much conquest, became Saudi Arabia's first king and, more generally, to the military triumphs of Islam. The modern flag is essentially that of 1906, although from time to time over the years the details of the sword have changed – to the extreme that for a while it was replaced by a pair of crossed swords.

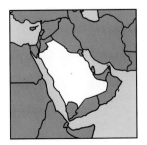

S

SENEGAL

Republic of
République du Sénégal

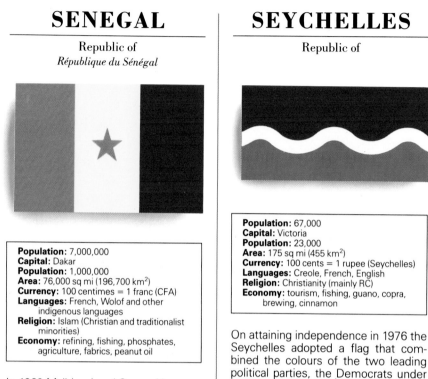

Population: 7,000,000
Capital: Dakar
Population: 1,000,000
Area: 76,000 sq mi (196,700 km²)
Currency: 100 centimes = 1 franc (CFA)
Languages: French, Wolof and other indigenous languages
Religion: Islam (Christian and traditionalist minorities)
Economy: refining, fishing, phosphates, agriculture, fabrics, peanut oil

In 1960 Mali (*q.v.*) and Senegal became independent together, having in the previous year federated – to form the Federation of Mali – and adopted a joint flag; shortly after independence the two nations agreed to go their separate ways, Mali keeping both name and flag. Senegal altered the flag simply by substituting a five-pointed green star for the central figure of the 1959 flag. The star expresses Pan-African unity, peace, hope and socialism.

SEYCHELLES

Republic of

Population: 67,000
Capital: Victoria
Population: 23,000
Area: 175 sq mi (455 km²)
Currency: 100 cents = 1 rupee (Seychelles)
Languages: Creole, French, English
Religion: Christianity (mainly RC)
Economy: tourism, fishing, guano, copra, brewing, cinnamon

On attaining independence in 1976 the Seychelles adopted a flag that combined the colours of the two leading political parties, the Democrats under their reputedly playboy leader (and first national president), James Mancham (1940–   ), and the Seychelles People's United Party, led by Albert René (1935–   ), who became the country's first prime minister and who, in 1977, ousted Mancham who was attending the Commonwealth Conference in London; the coup seems to have been as good-natured as coups can be, as Mancham continued to function as leader of the opposition. SPUP changed the flag immediately on entering office, substituting a design exactly similar to that of its own flag except for the omission of stylized rising sun of liberty. The meanings of the colours are said to be as follows: white for the waves and the resources of the Indian Ocean, green for agriculture and vegetation, and red for the customary mixture of blood, sweat, tears and revolutionary fervour.

SIERRA LEONE

Republic of

Population: 4,000,000
Capital: Freetown
Population: 300,000
Area: 28,000 sq mi (72,000 km²)
Currency: 100 cents = 1 leone
Languages: English, Krio, Mende, Temne
Religions: Animism, Islam, Christianity
Economy: agriculture, diamonds, bauxite, coffee, cocoa, fishing

The flag of Sierra Leone was adopted in 1961 when the country attained its independence from the UK. Blue is for the Atlantic, green for agriculture and white for peace, justice, virtue, unity and all the similar sentiments. The country's name, which means "lion mountain", was given to it by the Portuguese sailors who discovered the country in 1462, probably because one of the mountains on Cape Sierra Leone (the peninsula on which Freetown stands) can be perceived to resemble a crouching lion; a more fanciful explanation is that they mistook distant thunder for the roaring of giant lions. Whichever, lions feature prominently in the country's arms.

The arms of Senegal

SINGAPORE

Republic of
Republik Singapura

Population: 2,670,000
Capital: Singapore
Population: 2,530,000
Area: 240 sq mi (620 km²)
Currency: 100 cents = 1 dollar (Singapore)
Languages: Malaysian, Chinese, English, Tamil
Religions: Buddhism, Islam, Hinduism, Christianity, Taoism; also Confucianism
Economy: oil refining, machinery, rubber, international trade, coconuts, fruit, vegetables, fishing, electronics, electrical equipment, printing, ship-building and repairs

The Singapore flag, in the traditional Malaysian colours of red and white, was adopted in 1959 when the country attained self-government as a UK colony. Since then it has survived a period as part of the Federation of Malaysia, between 1963 and the country's secession in 1965, in which latter year Singapore gained full independence. The white is as ever for virtue and purity and the red for the universal fellowship of mankind. The crescent expresses the youth of the state, and the five five-pointed stars represent the five ideals through adherence to which the state hopes to make its future: democracy, peace, progress, justice and equality.

SLOVENIA

Slovenija

Population: 1,891,864
Capital: Ljubljana
Population: 306,000
Area: 7,817 sq mi (20,250 km²)
Language: Slovene (a Romanized variety of Serbo-Croat)
Religion: Roman Catholicism
Economy: cereals, sugarbeet, livestock, textiles, lumber, steel, motor vehicles, minerals, hydroelectricity, tourism, wine

Until 1918, when Yugoslavia (*q.v.*) was manufactured as the Kingdom of the Serbs, Croats and Slovenes, Slovenia was a province of Austria and called Carniola. It has been a unitary state since 1991, when it seceded from Yugoslavia after a short period of civil war which was less bloody than that suffered by Croatia (*q.v.*) – largely because Croatia acted as a buffer between Slovenia and the dominant Serbia. The colours of the flag are Slav.

SOLOMON ISLANDS

State of

Population: 300,000
Capital: Honiara
Population: 22,500
Area: 11,500 sq mi (29,800 km²)
Currency: 100 cents = 1 dollar (Solomon Islands)
Languages: English, Pidgin English, indigenous languages
Religions: Christianity, indigenous religions
Economy: agriculture, fishing, wood, copra

The result of official discussion and a design competition, the flag of the Solomon Islands was created in 1977 and adopted the following year. The five five-pointed stars on a background of blue represent the archipelagian nation's five administrative units surrounded by the Pacific (and not, as is sometimes claimed, its main islands, for of these there are six). The green is for vegetal lushness and the yellow for sunshine.

The arms of the Solomon Islands

S

75

SOMALIA

Somali Democratic Republic
al-Jumhouriya as-Somaliya al-Domocradia

Population: 7,110,000
Capital: Mogadishu (Mogadiscio, Muqdisho)
Population: 500,000
Area: 246,300 sq mi (638,000 km²)
Currency: 100 centesimi = 1 shilling (Somali)
Language: Somali
Religion: Islam
Economy: animal husbandry, meat, hides, skins, bananas, sugar, cotton

Adopted in 1950 by Italian Somaliland, then a UN Trust Territory, the flag was adopted in 1960 by the new country of Somalia, which was formed out of the Italian and British Somalilands. It is based on the United Nations flag, with which it shares its colours (although in the case of Somalia the blue is sometimes claimed to represent the bright sky). The star expresses the cause of African freedom, and its five points represent the five divisions into which history, geography and politics had sundered the Somali peoples: these five divisions were, in territorial terms, the Somalis of French Somaliland (now Djibouti, *q.v.*), British and Italian Somaliland, northern Kenya and Ethiopia.

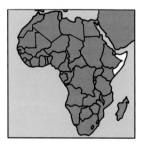

SOUTH AFRICA

Republic of
Republik van Suid Afrika/
Republic of South Africa

Population: 33,750,000
Capital: Pretoria
Population: 740,000
Area: 470,000 sq mi (1,220,000 km²)
Currency: 100 cents = 1 rand (SA)
Languages: Afrikaans, English, Bantu
Religions: Christianity, indigenous religions (Hindu, Islam and Jewish minorities)
Economy: gold, diamonds, metals, coal, fruit, agriculture, fishing, oil refining, machinery, chemicals

South Africa's current flag was introduced in 1928, and until 1957 it was always flown in conjunction with the Union Jack. It has the red-white-blue of the flag of the Netherlands, to which country many of the minority white population owe their ancestry. On the central stripe is superimposed an emblem made up out of the Union Jack and the flags of the Transvaal and the Orange Free State; the UK flag represents the two British colonies (Natal and Cape Province), which came together with the other two in 1961 to form the Union. The aim was to placate those of British and those of Dutch descent.

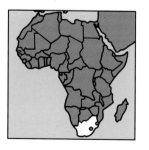

SPAIN

Kingdom of
Estado Español

Population: 39,100,000
Capital: Madrid
Population: 3,275,000
Area: 195,000 sq mi (505,000 km²)
Currency: 100 centimos = 1 peseta
Languages: Castilian, Catalan, Galician, Basque
Religion: Christianity (almost exclusively RC)
Economy: agriculture, machinery, automobiles, wine, fruit, metals, mining, oil refining, olive oil, textiles, shoes

If tradition is to be believed, the colours of Spain date back to the 9th century, when the French King Charles I the Bald (823–77) granted colours to the Count of Aragon by smearing his blood-stained hands on the latter's plain leather shield. Whatever the truth, certainly red and white stripes were the recognized sign of Aragon by the 12th century, and in 1793, with the arms of León and Castile, they were used in the national flag. During the short-lived First Republic of 1873–4 the lower red band was rendered in purple to expunge the reference to royalty, but by 1875 the original colour scheme was back. At the start of the Second Republic, in 1931, the purple was again deployed in a similar way; however, only a few years later, in 1936, the dictator Francisco Franco intervened to restore the old design except with, now, a new coat of arms in the yellow central band. In 1981, six years after his death, this was dropped.

SRI LANKA

Democratic Socialist Republic of
Janarajaya Sri Lanka

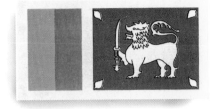

Population: 16,600,000
Capital: Colombo
Population: 625,000
Area: 25,300 sq mi (65,600 km²)
Currency: 100 cents = 1 rupee (Sri Lankan)
Languages: Sinhala, Tamil, English
Religions: Buddhism, Hinduism (Islamic and Christian minorities)
Economy: tea, rubber, rice, agriculture, coconuts, oil refining, gems, textiles, fruit, fishing

The symbol of the lion clutching a sword was adopted for the national flag when the country gained independence, as Ceylon, from the UK in 1948; with four attendant stylized pagodas, it had served as the flags of the kings of Kandy since ancient times. In 1951 the two vertical stripes were added to the flag to acknowledge the country's minority groups: orange for the Tamils (Hindus) and green for the Muslims. In 1972, when the country changed its name and declared itself a republic, the pagodas were replaced with stylized leaves from the sacred bo tree under which the Buddha meditated, and in 1978 the design of these leaves was modified towards greater realism.

SUDAN

Democratic Republic of the
Jamuryat es-Sudan

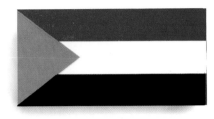

Population: 23,800,000
Capital: Khartoum
Population: 560,000
Area: 965,000 sq mi (2,500,000 km²)
Currency: 100 piastres = 1 pound (Sudanese)
Languages: Arabic, English, Nubian
Religions: Islam, indigenous religions (Christian minority)
Economy: cotton, agriculture, oil, gas, chromium

Like that of Jordan (*q.v.*) and others, the Sudanese flag is in the Pan-Arab colours of red, white, green and black. From 1899 until 1956 Sudan was an Anglo-Egyptian condominium. Independence brought with it a green, yellow and blue tricolour, which survived a military coup in 1958 and the restoration of civilian rule in 1964, but not the military coup of 1969, which brought to power the regime of the dictatorial President Jaafar Nimeiri (1929–), which held a design competition to determine a new flag; the winning design was adopted in 1970.

The arms of Sudan

SURINAM

Republic of
Republiek van Suriname

Population: 415,000
Capital: Paramaribo
Population: 165,000
Area: 63,000 sq mi (163,250 km²)
Currency: 100 cents = 1 guilder (Surinamese)
Languages: Dutch, English, Hindi, Javanese, Chinese, "Surinamese" (lingua franca)
Religions: Christianity, Hinduism, Islam
Economy: agriculture, bauxite, rice, wood, sugar, fruit

Surinam was English from 1650 until 1667, when it was ceded to the Netherlands in exchange for what was then New Amsterdam – in other words, New York. Despite occasional British occupations, the country was named Dutch Guiana until 1948; in the year after the change of name it was granted some measure of self-government, in 1954 it became internally self-governing, and finally in 1975 it became an independent republic, with a new flag which has remained unchanged since then. The dominant colours, red, green and white, represent the three main political groupings as well as having predictable subsidiary meanings (red for progress, etc.; green for agriculture, etc.; white for purity, etc.). The star has five points for the nation's five ethnic communities and is yellow as an expression of the golden future.

S

SWAZILAND

Kingdom of

Population: 740,000
Capital: Mbabane
Population: 30,000
Area: 6,700 sq mi (17,400 km²)
Currency: 100 cents = 1 lilangeni
Languages: English, Swazi
Religions: Christianity, indigenous religions
Economy: sugar, agriculture, wood, tourism, cotton, tobacco, mining, chemicals, asbestos

The Swaziland flag has a design very similar to one first given in 1941 to the Emasotsha regiment of the Swazi Pioneer Corps during the time the land was still British; it was adopted, virtually unchanged, when Swaziland became independent in 1968. The blue is for peace, the yellow for mineral resources and the red for battle. The shield is of oxhide and bears a tassel of royalty; the fighting staff beneath the two spears bears two of these tassels, which denote royalty.

The arms of Swaziland

SWEDEN

Kingdom of
Konungariket Sverige

Population: 8,450,000
Capital: Stockholm
Population: 1,385,000
Area: 174,000 sq mi (450,000 km²)
Currency: 100 öre = 1 krona
Language: Swedish
Religion: Christianity (almost exclusively Evangelical Lutheran)
Economy: engineering, dairy products, agriculture, wood and wood products, paper, automobiles, metals, chemicals

According to legend, the Danish King Valdemar II (1170–1241), whose life-long hobby was conquest, had a vision on the eve of the Battle of Lyndanisse of a white crucifix in the darkening sky; this he interpreted to mean that Christ wished him to triumph in slaughter on the morrow, which he duly did. Thus, so the story continues, was born the Scandinavian Cross, seen also in the flags of Finland, Iceland, Norway (*qq.v.*) and Sweden; the cross was originally square, but over the centuries one of its horizontals was extended. Although officially adopted only in 1906, the Swedish version of this basic design has a very long history. It seems to have been adopted about 1520 as the flag under which the Swedish nationalists fought against their Danish oppressors after their fervour had been kindled by the massacre of Stockholm. Led by Gustavus (1496–1560), they swiftly drove out the Danes, crowning their leader Gustavus Vasa in 1523. The colours came originally from the use in the national arms of three golden crowns on a blue background.

SWITZERLAND

Confederation of
Schweizerische Eidgenossenschaft/ Confédération Suisse/Confederazione Svizzera/Confederaziun Svizra

Population: 6,570,000
Capital: Berne (Bern)
Population: 144,000
Area: 15,950 sq mi (41,300 km²)
Currency: 100 centimes (Rappen) = 1 Swiss franc (Frank)
Languages: German, French, Italian, Romansch
Religion: Christianity
Economy: financial services, tourism, machinery, chemicals, pharmaceuticals, watches and clocks, precision instruments, textiles, agriculture

The Swiss flag is the only national flag to be square. In its current form it was adopted only in 1848 (revised in 1889), but it is of much greater antiquity than that. A form of it seems to have been in use in the canton of Schwyz by the end of the 13th century; in 1339 the federated cantons of Schwyz, Lucerne, Nidwalden and Uri adopted it as their common flag in their struggle for liberation from the Holy Roman Empire. The flag survived Switzerland's full independence in 1648, occupation by the French in 1798–1815, and ensuing religious strife that threatened to split the country; it has become a symbol for neutrality.

SYRIA

Syrian Arab Republic
al-Jamhouriya al-'Arabiya as Souriya

Population: 11,400,000
Capital: Damascus (Dimashq)
Population: 1,250,000
Area: 71,500 sq mi (185,200 km^2)
Currency: 100 piastres = 1 pound (Syrian)
Language: Arabic
Religion: Islam (Christian minority)
Economy: oil, gas, cotton, agriculture, mining, animal husbandry, minerals, textiles, fruit, wool

The flag of Syria is in the Pan-Arab colours, like that of Jordan (*q.v.*) and others, but without the black. When Egypt (*q.v.*) and Syria (and later North Yemen) formed the United Arab Republic in 1958, all three shared very similar flags, the Syrian version having two green stars on the central band of a red-white-green arrangement. In fact, Syria and North Yemen withdrew from the Republic almost immediately, in 1961, and for a couple of years Syria used an older flag. In 1963 it adopted a red-white-black arrangement with three green stars in the central band, thereby sharing the same flag as Iraq (*q.v.*), in the unfulfilled expectation that Egypt, Syria and Iraq would soon come together. When Libya, Egypt and Syria formed the short-lived Federation of Arab Republics in 1971, Syria replaced the three stars with a golden hawk. In 1980 it reverted to the flag first used in 1958.

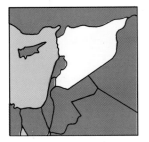

TAJIKISTAN

Tojokiston

Population: 4,500,000
Capital: Dushanbe
Population: 539,000
Area: 55,250 sq mi (143,100 km^2)
Languages: Tadzhik, Russian
Religion: Islam
Economy: cotton, cereals, fruit, livestock, minerals, textiles, engineering, mulberry farming (for silk), coal, oil, gas

Tajikistan has been a unitary state since 1991, having become so at the time of the general dissolution of the Union of Soviet Socialist Republics. The land is extremely mountainous; it contains the peak which was, before the collapse of the union, the highest in the USSR, Communism Peak, in the Pamir Range. Tajikistan's history is one of foreign domination – Alexander the Great was one of many to count it among his occupations. During the 16th century it was taken over by Bukhara (Bokhara), a powerful kingdom centred on what is now the Bukhara region of Uzbekistan (*q.v.*) and which was ceded to Russia in 1868.

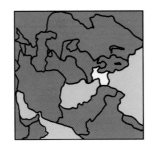

TAIWAN

Republic of China
Ta Çhunghwa Min-Kuo

Population: 19,700,000
Capital: T'ai-pei
Population: 2,300,000
Area: 13,800 sq mi (35,975 km^2)
Currency: 100 cents = 1 dollar (New Taiwanese)
Languages: Mandarin, Hakka, Hokkien
Religions: Buddhism, Taoism, Christianity, also Confucianism
Economy: electrical goods, electronics, textiles, clothing, assorted manufactured goods, chemicals, agriculture, fruit, coal

The flag of Taiwan is that adopted by the Guomindang government of Chiang Kai-shek (1887–1975) for China as a whole in 1928 (see page 28) and used as the national flag until the communist victory in the Chinese Civil War in 1949 and the subsequent Guomindang flight to the island of Taiwan; earlier the flag had been used by the Guomindang under Sun Yat-sen (1866–1925). The red is for the nation of China – just as it is in the flag of the People's Republic – and the small rectangle shows, against a blue sky, a white sun (representing the yang principle) whose 12 points stand for the hours of the day and of the night. (This may reflect the fact that the Chinese were – in the 4th century BC – probably the first civilization to develop an equal-hour timekeeping system like our modern one, rather than using temporal hours, which were divisions of the periods of daylight and darkness into 12 and thus varied in duration throughout the year.)

T

TANZANIA

United Republic of

Population: 24,000,000
Capital: Dar es Salaam
Population: 850,000
Area: 365,000 sq mi (945,000 km²)
Currency: 100 cents = 1 shilling (Tanzanian)
Languages: Swahili, English
Religions: Christianity, Islam, indigenous religions (Hindu minority)
Economy: cotton, agriculture, coffee, sisal, diamonds, textiles, oil refining, coconuts

Adopted in 1964 when Tanganyika united with Zanzibar to become Tanzania, the flag combines elements from those adopted by the two countries on attainment of their individual independences, Tanganyika in 1961 and Zanzibar in 1963 – the latter country shortly after independence and just before the union deposing its sultan. The colours of the leading Tanganyikan political party, the Tanganyika African National Union, were green and black – the flag had also thin yellow stripes – and those of its counterpart in Zanzibar, the Afro-Shirazi Party, were blue, black and green. The yellow stripes survived in the new flag, which otherwise included the colours of both parties in bands set diagonally to forestall any questions of ranking. The meanings of the colours are said to be green for agriculture, black for the people and blue for the sea, with the yellow veins referring to the nation's mineral resources.

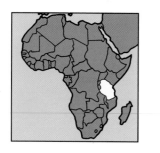

THAILAND

Kingdom of
Prathes Thai/Muang-Thai

Population: 54,550,000
Capital: Bangkok (Krung Thep)
Population: 5,500,000
Area: 200,000 sq mi (515,000 km²)
Currency: 100 satang = 1 baht
Language: Thai
Religion: Buddhism (Islamic minority)
Economy: rice, agriculture, tapioca, rubber, textiles, clothing, tin, sugar, maize

During the 19th century the Thai flag featured a white elephant, one of the symbols of both the country itself ("The Land of the White Elephant") and its monarchs ("The Kings of the White Elephant"). In the latter part of the century the flag was plain red with a central white elephant; in 1916 horizontal white stripes above and below the beast were introduced; and in 1917 the animal was omitted altogether. Later that year, as a gesture of solidarity with the Allies in World War I, a central blue band was inserted so that the colours matched those of the French flag.

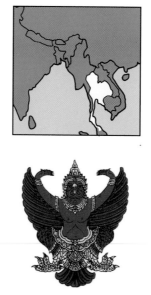

The emblem of Thailand

TOGO

Republic of
République Togolaise

Population: 3,250,000
Capital: Lomé
Population: 240,000
Area: 22,000 sq mi (56,750 km²)
Currency: 100 centimes = 1 franc (CFA)
Languages: French, Ewe, Kabra, indigenous languages
Religions: indigenous religions, Christianity, Islam
Economy: phosphates, agriculture, cocoa, coffee, textiles

Introduced in 1960 when the country gained its independence, the flag of Togo, which is in the Pan-African colours, seems to have been inspired to some measure by the Stars and Stripes or by one of its imitators. The five stripes represent the republic's five major administrative units; the white star is for purity, unity and the bright inspiration of progress; yellow is for mineral reserves; green for agriculture and vegetal abundance; and red is for bloodshed, patriotic fervour and fidelity.

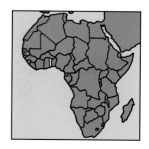

TOKELAU
See New Zealand

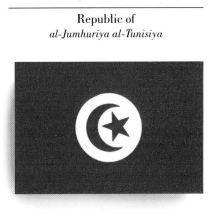

T

TONGA

Kingdom of
Pule'ange Tonga/Kingdom of Tonga

Population: 116,000
Capital: Nuku'alofa
Population: 21,000
Area: 290 sq mi (750 km²)
Currency: 100 seniti = 1 pa'anga
Languages: Tongan, English
Religion: Christianity (mainly Protestant)
Economy: copra, coconuts, vanilla, fruit, taro, fishing

The design of the flag of Tonga was established as inalterable in the first national constitution in 1875 at the express behest of King Taufa'ahau Tupou George I (1797–1893), who wished the flag to reflect his own — and, he hoped, his subjects' — devotion to Christianity; in fact, the flag was in use for about a decade before its constitutional adoption. Because of the monarch's keystone role in the nation's history, there has been no move to amend this aspect of the constitution; the red cross itself has become Tonga's national emblem. Based on the British Red Ensign, the flag has further Christian symbolism in that its red is for the blood of Christ shed on the cross.

TRINIDAD AND TOBAGO

Republic of

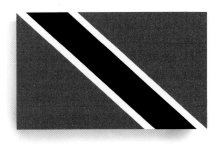

Population: 1,245,000
Capital: Port of Spain
Population: 66,000
Area: 1,980 sq mi (5130 km²)
Currency: 100 cents = 1 dollar (Trinidad and Tobago)
Languages: English, Hindi, French, Spanish
Religions: Christianity, Hinduism, (Islamic minority)
Economy: oil, tourism, sugar, chemicals, agriculture, cocoa, coffee, fruit

The flag of Trinidad and Tobago was adopted in 1962 when the country gained its independence and survived unchanged when the nation became a republic in 1976. The design has no obvious symbolism (it was determined by a committee). The colours were selected for various reasons: black is for the islands' wealth, for their inhabitants' fortitude and for those inhabitants themselves; red is for the warmth and vitality of the sun, the people and the nation; and white is for purity, emancipation and the waves breaking on the nation's shores.

TUNISIA

Republic of
al-Jumhuriya al-Tunisiya

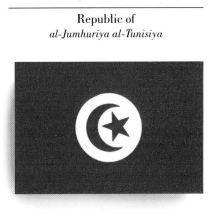

Population: 7,810,000
Capital: Tunis
Population: 600,000
Area: 63,200 sq mi (163,700 km²)
Currency: 1000 millimes = 1 dinar
Languages: Arabic, French
Religion: Islam (Jewish and Christian minorities)
Economy: agriculture, oil, gas, phosphates, textiles, chemicals, fishing, wine

The flag of Turkey (*q.v.*) was in widespread use in Tunisia from about the beginning of the 19th century, and in 1835 a version of it was introduced that has survived more or less unchanged until today. On Tunisia's attainment of independence from the French the flag became the national flag. The symbolism is as for the Turkish flag except for the inclusion of a white circle representing the sun.

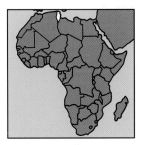

The arms of Tunisia

TURKEY

Republic of
Türkiya Cumhuriyeti

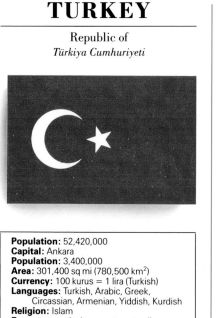

Population: 52,420,000
Capital: Ankara
Population: 3,400,000
Area: 301,400 sq mi (780,500 km²)
Currency: 100 kurus = 1 lira (Turkish)
Languages: Turkish, Arabic, Greek,
Circassian, Armenian, Yiddish, Kurdish
Religion: Islam
Economy: agriculture, cotton, textiles,
nuts, fruit, coal, metals, oil refining

The crescent moon and the star are ancient symbols – and red a colour – of both Islam and, more specifically, of Turkey and the Ottoman Empire. Ottoman flags bearing the crescent symbol are known from as early as the 16th century, and in 1793 the crescent and star appeared for the first time together on the Turkish flag – although the star had six rather than the now more customary five points. For a short period in the early 1920s the flag was Islamic green, but on the declaration of the republic under Kemal Atatürk (1881–1938) it reverted to red. Paradoxically, red has also been used as a token of Arab resistance to Turkish oppression. The emblem of the crescent and star has been adopted by numerous other Islamic countries, although the precise arrangement – one apex of the star lying exactly on the imaginary straight line joining the two cusps – has nowhere been exactly copied except in the quasi-official flag of the Turkish community in Cyprus (*q.v.*).

TURKMENIA

Tiurkmenostan

Population: 3,200,000
Capital: Aschabad (Ashkhabad)
Population: 356,000
Area: 188,455 sq mi (488,100 km²)
Languages: Turkoman (one of the Turkic
group), Russian
Religion: Islam
Economy: sheep, karakul pelts, fruit,
cotton, cereals, oil, gas, sulphur, silk

Turkmenia has been a unitary state since 1991, having become so at the time of the general dissolution of the Union of Soviet Socialist Republics. Of the land, about 90 per cent is desert, notably the vast Kara Kum Desert (area about 118,500 sq mi/300,000 km²). For some reason, numerous outside powers have chosen over the centuries to invade Turkmenia; the modern republic was established within the USSR in 1925.

TURKS AND CAICOS ISLANDS
See United Kingdom

TUVALU

State of

Population: 9,700
Capital: Funafuti (Vaiaku)
Population: 830
Area: 10 sq mi (26 km²)
Currency: 100 cents = 1 dollar (Tuvaluan
and Australian)
Languages: Tuvaluan, English
Religion: Christianity (mainly Protestant)
Economy: postage stamps, copra, fishing,
fruit

As the Ellice Islands, Tuvalu was until 1975 part of the UK colony of the Gilbert and Ellice Islands; in that year it was separated from the Gilberts (now Kiribati, *q.v.*) as Tuvalu, and in 1978 it became an independent state and adopted a new flag based on a competition-winning design. The UK past is very evident, for this is essentially the Blue Ensign but done in a very pale blue (as in the flag of Fiji, *q.v.*). The nine golden stars represent the state's nine major islands, and their disposition is the same as that of the islands in the ocean (but with west at the top of the flag).

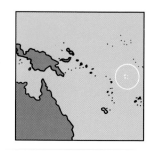

FAR LEFT **Cliff homes cut into sandstone in central Turkey. The Republic of Turkey is the only Middle Eastern country that is partly in Europe.**

U

UGANDA

Republic of

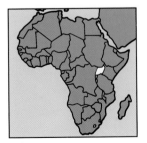

Population: 17,200,000
Capital: Kampala
Population: 460,000
Area: 91,100 sq mi (236,000 km²)
Currency: 100 cents = 1 shilling (Ugandan)
Languages: English, Swahili, Bantu, Luganda
Religions: Christianity, Islam
Economy: coffee, tea, cotton, sugar, copper, phosphates, automobiles

Just before Uganda gained its independence in 1962, the Democratic Party unexpectedly lost power to the Uganda People's Congress Party led by Milton Obote (1925–   ), who duly became the country's first prime minister. Unfortunately, a new national flag had already been prepared in the colours of the Democratic Party, and so some rapid work had to be done to create a revised version, in the UPC colours of black (for the people and for Africa), yellow (for the sun) and red (for universal fraternity), in time for the great occasion. The badge in the centre shows a crested crane on a white disc, a long-standing emblem of the country.

UKRAINE

Little Russia
Ukraina

Population: 51,704,000
Capital: Kiev
Population: 2,411,000
Area: 233,000 sq mi (603,700 km²)
Languages: Ukrainian, Russian
Religion: Christianity
Economy: cereals, sugarbeet, sunflowers, cotton, vegetables, milk, meat, food processing, coal, heavy machinery, chemicals, iron and steel

Ukraine has been a unitary state since 1991, having become so at the time of the general dissolution of the Union of Soviet Socialist Republics. It was the third largest of the republics of the old USSR and second only to the Russian Federation (*q.v.*) in terms of population, industrial production and agricultural output; since the USSR's dissolution this near-equality in importance has led to a fair amount of jockeying for prestige between the two countries. Much of the nation's agricultural land suffered from radioactive fallout in the wake of the 1986 Chernobyl disaster, the mismanagement of which did little to endear to the Ukrainians the concept of union with the Russians. Ukraine's previous period of independence (excluding a part ruled by Poland from 1919) lasted only from 1918 to 1922, when it became part of the USSR; even then, the part of it that had been ruled by Poland remained so until 1939. Along with Belorussia (*q.v.*), it was one of only two of the USSR's republics to have a separate vote at the UN.

UNITED ARAB EMIRATES

Dawlat al-Imārāt al-ʾArabīya al-Muttahida

Population: 1,500,000
Capital: Abu Dhabi (Abu Zaby)
Population: 243,000
Area: 32,630 sq mi (83,660 km²)
Currency: 100 fils = 1 dirham
Languages: Arabic, English
Religion: Islam
Economy: oil, gas, animal husbandry, agriculture, fishing

Like the flag of Jordan (*q.v.*) and others, that of the United Arab Emirates is in the Pan-Arab colours. The sheikdoms that came together in 1971 in this federation – Abu Dhabi, Ajman, Dubai, Fujairah, Ras al-Khaimah (joined 1972), Sharjah and Umm al-Qaiwain – had all (except Fujairah) been among those Gulf states that, in 1820, signed an agreement with the British to add white to their traditional plain red flags of the Kharidjite sect of Islam, to distinguish their vessels from pirate ones; from 1892 they were UK protectorates as the Trucial States. On independence they chose the Pan-Arab colours but with the red band placed vertically as a reminder of their Kharidjite flag.

UNITED KINGDOM OF GREAT BRITAIN AND NORTHERN IRELAND

Population: 57,100,000
Capital: London
Population: 6,735,400
Area: 94,250 sq mi (244,100 km²)
Currency: 100 pence = 1 pound (sterling)
Languages: English, Gaelic, Welsh, Cornish, Erse
Religion: Christianity (mainly Protestant) (Islamic, Jewish, Hindu and Sikh minorities)
Economy: agriculture, oil, gas, coal, chemicals, automobiles, manufactured goods, armaments, textiles, processed foods, paper, financial services, tourism

The national flag of the United Kingdom is the Union Flag, more commonly known as the Union Jack and, along with the Stars and Stripes and the French tricolour, it is one of the best known flags in the world. It was adopted in 1801 and has remained unchanged. It is made up from the crosses of St George (England) and St Andrew (Scotland) and a cross, generally called St Patrick's Cross, of the powerful Geraldine family of Ireland. The earliest form of the flag was introduced in 1606, three years after James VI of Scotland (1566–1625) had succeeded Elizabeth I of England (1533–1603) to become King James I of Scotland and England. It was formed by superimposing the Cross of St George on the Cross of St Andrew, using the latter's blue background also for the flag as a whole except for a thin white edging of the St George's Cross, red on blue being a heraldic taboo. During the Commonwealth, from 1649, Oliver Cromwell (1599–1658) further superimposed the image of a gaelic harp on the whole to register his brutal conquest of Ireland, but this was

dropped on the Restoration of the Monarchy in 1660. In 1707 came the Act of Union, the legislative incorporation of England and Scotland, and Queen Anne (1665–1714) approved the original flag for use on land and at sea in all flags, standards, ensigns and banners. 1800 saw the union with Ireland, and from the time this came into effect, at the beginning of 1801, the new version of the Union Jack was adopted. This integrates the arms of the red Cross of St Patrick with those of the white Cross of St Andrew in such a way that neither is seen to be superior to the other, the red stripes being placed above the white stripes in the right-hand quarters and below them in the left-hand quarters. The modern flag is authorized for use only on land and by land forces. At sea it may be flown only by a craft bearing the monarch or by the flagship of a fleet commanded by an admiral. For all other uses at sea the design must be incorporated as the top left-hand corner of an otherwise plain red or blue or white flag – called, respectively, the Red Ensign (for merchant ships) and the Blue Ensign (for the Royal Naval Reserve) – or on a Cross of St George – the White Ensign (used by warships and, from 1864, reserved exclusively for the Royal Navy). The ensign used by the Royal Air Force has a pale blue background and incorporates the RAF emblem of a red, white and blue target. Adaptations of the ensigns have been adopted by various Commonwealth countries and UK dependencies and territories, by some Canadian and all the Australian states. The Union Flag appears also in the flag of one state of the USA (q.v.), Hawaii, but this is for rather different reasons.

England

Population: 47,540,000
Capital: London
Population: 6,735,400
Area: 50,800 sq mi (130,400 km²)

The Cross of St George seems to have originated during the Crusades; in due course it became widely popular in England and soon came to be used as the national flag (it remained in use in some official contexts as late as 1824). Its early popularity derived from the cult of St George, brought back to England from Palestine by the Crusaders. Of dubious historical status, St George was said to have been a martyr at Nicomedia in AD303 under Diocletian (245–313). His dragon-slaying exploit seems to have been an invention of the Italian hagiographer Jacobus de Voragine (1230–98).

A version of the Cross of St George is today used by the International Red Cross, an organization founded by the Geneva Convention of 1864; however, this emblem should more correctly be interpreted as being the flag of Switzerland (q.v.) with the colours reversed. In 1876 it was accepted that Muslims might understandably misinterpret the design as a Christian one and take justifiable offence; a second design, the Red Crescent, with an exactly similar meaning, was therefore recognized.

Scotland

Population: 5,100,000
Capital: Edinburgh
Population: 433,500
Area: 30,400 sq mi (78,300 km²)

UK – COUNTRIES

The Cross of St Andrew, or the Saltire, is today widely used to represent Scotland at sporting contests and the like, and by the Scottish National Party; it is also permitted to be used by Scottish vessels in place of the Red Ensign, although this is nowadays rare. Its origins are obscure and seem to have little to do with the apostle Andrew, who is patron saint not only of Scotland but also of Russia. The belief that the cross on which he was crucified was diagonal rather than upright seems to date only from the 14th century.

Wales

Population: 2,860,000
Capital: Cardiff
Population: 283,900
Area: 8,100 sq mi (20,760 km^2)

The Welsh flag is known as *Y Ddraig Goch* ("The Red Dragon"), and was officially adopted as late as 1958. The dragon is said to have been the emblem of the Welsh Prince Cadwaladr (d1172), who resisted the forces of Henry II of England (1133–89) despite having been blinded. Green and white were the colours of the princes of Gwynedd (hence the adoption of the leek as a national emblem), and it is said that the famous Welsh chief Owen Glyndwr or Glendower (*c*1350–*c*1416) – depicted by Shakespeare in *Henry IV* – used a form of the current flag during his guerrilla warfare against the English. These colours were also adopted by the Tudors, so the flag can be seen as a fusion of a large part Welsh with a small part English.

RIGHT An etching showing the Act of Union of 1707, read before Queen Anne, which saw the legislative incorporation of England and Scotland.

Northern Ireland

Population: 1,580,000
Capital: Belfast
Population: 299,600
Area: 5,260 sq mi (13,480 km^2)

Although the official flag of Ulster is currently the Union Jack, loyalists to the UK still make use of the flag that was adopted by the Northern Irish Government in 1953 and that had official status until 1972 and the reimposition of direct rule from London. The star has six points to acknowledge the six counties of the province, and the crown is that of the UK. The central emblem, commonly known as the Red Hand of Ulster, is more correctly termed the Red Hand of the O'Neills. That family can be traced back to Con O'Neill (*c*1484–*c*1559) and, paradoxically in view of the loyalist use of the symbol, is most noted for the wars and rebellions it waged throughout most of the 15th and 16th centuries against the English and Scots.

The so-called Cross of St Patrick has nothing to do with the saint; St Patrick (*c*385–*c*461) was not a martyr and so has never been represented by a cross. And "his" cross has never in fact been used on any form of national Irish flag, being rather the symbol of the Geraldine (Fitzgerald) family, who were sent by Henry II of England to suppress Ireland rather than to espouse its cause.

U

THE ACT OF UNION READ BEFORE QUEEN ANNE.

UK – ASSOCIATED LANDS

Channel Islands

Jersey

Guernsey

Population: 130,000
Area: 77 sq mi (197 km²)

Jersey, Guernsey, Alderney, Herm and Sark, the latter three being dependencies of Guernsey, have individual flags. The flag of Jersey has the Cross of St Patrick with the English arms in the upper triangle. The flag of Guernsey was until 1985 the Cross of St George; in that year a yellow cross was superimposed on the red. The Alderney, Herm and Sark flags are all based on the Cross of St George: in the case of Alderney, the island's badge is superimposed on the cross's intersection; Herm has the island arms (featuring dolphins and monks) in the top left corner; and in that position Sark has the Norman arms (featuring two golden lions).

Isle of Man

Population: 64,300
Capital: Douglas
Population: 20,000
Area: 223 sq mi (572 km²)

The flag of this self-governing dependency incorporates an ancient three-legged symbol called the *trinacria*, whose origins are obscure but may be Viking, as may be those of a rather different form of the symbol used in Sicily – the Latin name of which island was as a result Trinacria.

Anguilla

Population: 6,700
Capital: The Valley
Population: 2,000
Area: 35 sq mi (90 km²)
Economy: vegetables, fruit, fishing, cattle

Until 1980 Anguilla was, with St Kitts-Nevis (*q.v.*), part of the Commonwealth associated state of St Kitts-Nevis-Anguilla; it then reverted to being a UK dependency. The three dolphins symbolize strength and stamina, the blue stripe youth and hope, and the broad white stripe peace.

Bermuda

Population: 57,800
Capital: Hamilton
Population: 1,600
Area: 20 sq mi (53 km²)
Economy: tourism, vegetables, fruit, tobacco, flowers, fishing

The current Bermudan flag dates from 1915, and it is the Red Ensign with the shield from the islands' arms. Held by a red lion is a depiction of the wreck in 1609 on the shores of the main island of the *Sea Venture*, captained by Sir George Somers (1554–1610), whose discovery of the islands – known for some time as the Somers Islands – led to their colonization from Virginia.

British Virgin Islands

Population: 13,300
Capital: Road Town
Population: 3,700
Area: 60 sq mi (153 km²)
Economy: tourism, rum, cattle, fishing, fruit, vegetables

The British Virgin Islands uses the Blue Ensign with the badge of the islands, dating from 1960 and depicting the wise virgin of the parable in *Matthew* along with her 12 lamps. The islands were named for her by Columbus, who discovered and claimed them early in his voyage of 1493–6.

Cayman Islands

Population: 25,000
Capital: Georgetown
Population: 7,900
Area: 98 sq mi (255 km²)
Economy: international finance, tourism, fishing

The flag of the Cayman Islands is the Blue Ensign with the arms in a white disc. Dating from 1958, these have a shield showing wavy blue and white lines for the sea, a single English lion and three stars to represent the three islands. Atop the shield is a turtle bearing a pineapple, and on a scroll beneath it is the motto "He Hath Founded It up on the Seas".

UK – ASSOCIATED LANDS

Falkland Islands

Population: 3,800
Capital: Port Stanley
Population: 1,200
Area: 4,700 sq mi (12,175 km²)
Economy: animal husbandry, wool, skins, fishing

Known by Argentina, which claims them, as the Malvinas, the Falkland Islands fly the Blue Ensign with the shield (which dates from 1948) on a white disc. The shield shows a ram above wavy blue and white lines, representing the sea, and a depiction of the *Desire*, the ship in which the English mariner John Davis or Davys (*c*1550–1605), in seeking the Magellan Strait in 1592, discovered the Falklands. Beneath the shield is a scroll bearing the motto "Desire the Right".

Gibraltar

Population: 30,000
Capital: Gibraltar Town
Population: 27,000
Area: 2.5 sq mi (6.5 km²)
Economy: tourism, ship repairs, harbourage

At sea Gibraltar uses the Blue Ensign with the city arms, officially adopted as late as 1936 by the UK but originally granted by Ferdinand and Isabella of Spain in 1502. On land the Union Jack is the official flag, but more commonly the flag used is one made legal in 1982 and having a red band beneath a broad white one; on this arrangement is superimposed a part of the arms showing a stylized castle from whose main gate depends a golden key, expressing the fact that Gibraltar is the "gateway" to the Mediterranean.

Hong Kong

Population: 5,700,000
Capital: Victoria
Population: 635,000
Area: 404 sq mi (1,045 km²)
Economy: manufactured (especially plastic) goods, electronics, watches and clocks

The flag of Hong Kong, adopted in 1959 and destined to survive until the colony comes under Chinese rule in 1997, is the Blue Ensign with the colony's arms on a white disc. The arms have a Chinese dragon and a British lion supporting a shield on which are depicted two junks at sea.

Montserrat

Population: 13,200
Capital: Plymouth
Population: 3,600
Area: 39 sq mi (101 km²)
Economy: cotton, vegetables, bananas, coconuts, dairy produce

Adopted in 1960 after being administratively separated from the Leeward Islands, the Montserrat flag is the Blue Ensign with the colony's badge, which shows a female figure holding a golden harp and a Passion cross.

Pitcairn Island

Population: 65 (approx.)
Capital: Adamstown
Area: 14.5 sq mi (37.5 km²)
Economy: fruit and vegetables

Colonized in 1790 after the mutiny on the *Bounty* by Fletcher Christian and eight of the other mutineers along with a number of Tahitian women, Pitcairn Island (the other three islands of the group are uninhabited) has, since 1984, flown the Blue Ensign with the dependency's arms. These show a shield surrounded by a wreath in green and gold and topped by a helmet bearing a wheelbarrow from which grows the shoot of a breadfruit tree. On the shield itself are depicted a copy of the Bible and the *Bounty*'s anchor.

St Helena and Dependencies

Population: 6,900
Capital: Jamestown
Population: 1,900
Area: 123 sq mi (315 km²)
Economy: hemp, vegetables, cattle, yams

The flag is the Blue Ensign with the shield from the dependency's arms, granted in 1984. On the shield is depicted a three-masted East Indiaman flying the Cross of St George as it sails between two volcanic outcrops.

Turks and Caicos Islands

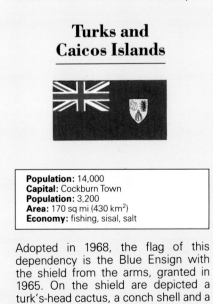

Population: 14,000
Capital: Cockburn Town
Population: 3,200
Area: 170 sq mi (430 km²)
Economy: fishing, sisal, salt

Adopted in 1968, the flag of this dependency is the Blue Ensign with the shield from the arms, granted in 1965. On the shield are depicted a turk's-head cactus, a conch shell and a spiny lobster.

U

UNITED STATES OF AMERICA

Population: 247,100,000
Capital: Washington D.C.
Population: 623,000
Area: 3,620,000 sq mi (9,375,000 km²)
Currency: 100 cents = 1 dollar (US)
Languages: English, numerous others
Religion: Christianity (Jewish and Islamic minorities)
Economy: agriculture, manufactured goods, electronics, electrical equipment, automobiles, chemicals, cereals, entertainment, armaments, publishing, textiles, aircraft, oil, gas, coal, metals, telecommunications equipment, paper and other wood products, fruit, vegetables, sugar, wine, tobacco

Possibly the most famous flag in the world, the Stars and Stripes (known also as Old Glory and as the Star-Spangled Banner) has a field of 13 alternating stripes of red and white (seven red, six white), representing the 13 original states, and a blue canton containing 50 stars, representing the 50 States of the Union. The original version of the flag was adopted on 14 June 1777, replacing a variety of revolutionary flags including the Grand Union Flag (or Continental Colours), first raised at the beginning of 1776 by George Washington (1732–99) in pro-claiming the organization of the Con-tinental Army; this flag had the 13 stripes but a Union Jack in the canton. Between 1795 and 1818 the number of both stripes and stars was 15, acknow-ledging the admission of Vermont and Kentucky; in 1818, however, Congress determined that in future the number of stripes should be restricted to 13 – but that a new star should be added to recognize each new state on the 4 July succeeding its admission. The origins of the Stars and Stripes' design are obscure, only later did sentimentality give rise to popular and usually falla-cious explanations. By far the most popular story concerns Elizabeth (Betsy) Ross (1752–1836), a flagmaker of Philadelphia. Her grandson, William

J. Canby, basing his story on family traditions, from 1870 claimed that she was asked in June 1776 by a committee of Congress (including Washington himself) to stitch the first Stars and Stripes from a sketch they supplied to her. However, there is no record of Congress having made any decisions concerning the independence flag before 1777 and, while examples are not unknown, it seems unlikely that a symbol of independence would be commissioned so far in advance of the declaration of that independence. Another and more plausible claim is that of Francis Hopkinson (1737–91), a signatory of the Declaration of Independence, who in 1780 billed Congress for having designed the flag. Although Congress declined to pay his bill on the grounds that many people had contributed to the design, it did not straightforwardly rebut his claim.

The law of 1818 stipulating the number of stripes and the timing of addition of future stars provided only a general description of the flag, and various versions were created over the years. Precise colours varied, but more importantly so did the arrangement of the stars – they were usually in rows but could be in a circle or arranged to form a larger star; during the American Civil War the stars were often in gold rather than white. Not until 1912 was the design officially standardized (with revisions in 1959 and 1960 to accommodate Alaska and Hawaii, res-pectively). In 1942 Congress brought into law a precise code of etiquette for use in conjunction with the flag governing such practices as the speed of its raising and lowering and its dis-play on or near every schoolhouse on schooldays. In 1953 this code was amended to permit the UN flag to be flown above the Stars and Stripes.

It was the flag with 15 stars and 15 stripes that during the War of 1812 was flying over Fort McHenry in Balti-more Harbor on the night of 13 September 1813 and inspired Francis Scott Key (1779–1843) to write "The Star-Spangled Banner", which in 1931 by Act of Congress became the US national anthem.

Alabama

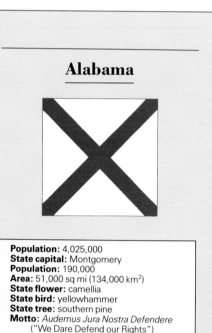

Population: 4,025,000
State capital: Montgomery
Population: 190,000
Area: 51,000 sq mi (134,000 km²)
State flower: camellia
State bird: yellowhammer
State tree: southern pine
Motto: *Audemus Jura Nostra Defendere* ("We Dare Defend our Rights")

Alabama was the 22nd State of the Union (14 December 1819). Unusually square, its flag – a crimson cross on a white background – is deliberately reminiscent of the Confederate States' Battle Flag. It was adopted in 1895.

Alaska

Population: 521,000
State capital: Juneau
Population: 24,000
Area: 586,400 sq mi (1,520,000 km²)
State flower: forget-me-not
State bird: willow ptarmigan
State tree: sitka spruce
Motto: North to the Future

Alaska was the 49th State of the Union (3 January 1959). Its flag, adopted in 1927 (well before statehood) shows the Plough (or Big Dipper) – part of the constellation Ursa Major – as well as Polaris, the northern pole star. The stars are golden, to represent Alaska's resources of that metal. The design, a competition winner, was by a 13-year-old Amerindian schoolboy.

USA – STATES OF THE UNION

Arizona

Population: 3,140,000
State capital: Phoenix
Population: 858,000
Area: 114,000 sq mi (295,000 km²)
State flower: saguaro (giant cactus)
State bird: cactus wren
State tree: paloverde
Motto: *Didat Deus* ("God Enriches")

Arizona was the 48th State of the Union (14 February 1912). Dominated by a very stylized image of sunrise over the desert, the Arizona flag, adopted in 1917, shows also a copper star as a representation of the state's mineral reserves. The 13 rays of the sunburst are for the 13 original states. The gold and red are the colours of Spain (*q.v.*), referring to the time when Arizona was under Spanish control.

Arkansas

Population: 2,360,000
State capital: Little Rock
Population: 171,000
Area: 53,100 sq mi (137,540 km²)
State flower: apple blossom
State bird: mockingbird
State tree: pine
Motto: *Regnat Populus* (The People Rule")

Arkansas was the 25th State of the Union (15 June 1836). Adopted in 1913 and modified in 1924, the state's flag has in its central diamond (Arkansas is a major diamond-producing state) four stars, one separated from the other three by the name Arkansas; this symbolizes the three powers that have ruled Arkansas – France, Spain and now the USA. There are 25 stars to indicate that Arkansas was the 25th state.

California

Population: 26,365,000
State capital: Sacramento
Population: 305,000
Area: 158,700 sq mi (411,000 km²)
State flower: golden poppy
State bird: California valley quail
State tree: California redwood
Motto: Eureka!

California was the 31st State of the Union (9 September 1850). The modern version of the flag, adopted in 1911, is a revision of the one created in 1846 for the short-lived California Republic. The bear is a grizzly and the star is for freedom; on the state seal the grizzly bear is employed as a symbol of the state itself.

This painting depicts patriot and flagmaker Betsy Ross holding the American flag.

U

USA – STATES OF THE UNION

Colorado

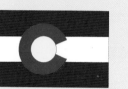

Population: 3,230,000
State capital: Denver
Population: 505,000
Area: 104,250 sq mi (270,000 km²)
State flower: Rocky Mountain columbine
State bird: lark bunting
State tree: Colorado blue spruce
Motto: *Nil Sine Numine* ("Nothing Without Providence")

Colorado was the 38th State of the Union (1 August 1876). Adopted in 1911 and revised in 1929 and 1964, the flag has a bold "C" for Colorado – the Spanish for "coloured red" – in the Spanish colours of gold and red, the golden ball representing the state's production of that metal. The blue and white of the rest of the flag derive (depending on opinion) either from the colours of the state flower, the Rocky Mountain columbine, or from the blue of the clear skies and the white of the snows on its mountains.

Connecticut

Population: 3,175,000
State capital: Hartford
Population: 136,000
Area: 5,010 sq mi (12,975 km²)
State flower: mountain laurel
State bird: American robin
State tree: white oak
Motto: *Qui Transtulit Sustinet* ("He Who Transplanted Us Still Sustains Us")

Connecticut was the 5th State of the Union (9 January 1788). The arms in the centre of the flag – which was adopted in 1897 for the state but dates back much earlier – are the colonial arms and show three vines in a shield; the vines symbolize the colony brought from the Old World and transplanted into the wilderness, a horticultural imagery perpetuated in the state's motto, which is given on the scroll.

Delaware

Population: 622,000
State capital: Dover
Population: 23,000
Area: 2,060 sq mi (5,330 km²)
State flower: peach blossom
State bird: blue hen chicken
State tree: American holly
Motto: Liberty and Independence

Delaware was the 1st State of the Union (7 December 1787); the date of its ratification of the US Constitution is proudly displayed on the flag. The buff lozenge with the state arms was added to a plain blue flag in 1913. The arms show a shield that bears a wheatsheaf, an ear of corn and an ox; a soldier and a farmer support the shield, and above it is the image of a sailing ship.

Florida

Population: 11,370,000
State capital: Tallahassee
Population: 115,000
Area: 58,560 sq mi (151,670 km²)
State flower: orange blossom
State bird: mockingbird
State tree: sabal palmetto
Motto: In God We Trust

Florida was the 27th State of the Union (3 March 1845). The flag it adopted in 1868 had the state seal in the centre of a plain white flag; the red cross – reminiscent of the Confederate States' Battle Flag – was added in 1899. Depicted in the seal, which was revised in 1985, is a Florida Indian maiden strewing flowers near a sabal palmetto with a Florida steamboat back-lit by the rising sun.

The arms of the USA

USA – STATES OF THE UNION

Georgia

Population: 5,840,000
State capital: Atlanta
Population: 430,000
Area: 58,890 sq mi (152,500 km²)
State flower: Cherokee rose
State bird: brown thrasher
State tree: live oak
Motto: Wisdom, Justice and Moderation

Georgia was the 4th State of the Union (2 January 1788). The current flag dates from 1956 and echoes the Confederate States' Battle Flag in its use of a diagonal cross with stars along the bars. The state seal shows a soldier standing, sword drawn, within a three-pillared archway; around the pillars is scrolled the state motto and over the arch appears the word "Constitution", to make it thoroughly clear what the soldier is defending.

Hawaii

Population: 1,055,000
State capital: Honolulu
Population: 375,000
Area: 6,450 sq mi (16,700 km²)
State flower: hibiscus
State bird: né-né (Hawaiin goose)
State tree: kukai (candlenut)
Motto: *Ua mau ke ea o ka aina i ka pono* ("The Life of the Land is Perpetuated in Righteousness")

Hawaii was the 50th and most recent State of the Union (21 August 1959). The Union Jack at top left does not denote any UK allegiance but a gift of a Union Jack by George Vancouver (*c*1758–98) in 1793 to the islands' then king, Kamehameha I (*c*1758–1819), who liked it so much that it was used as Hawaii's official flag until 1816. Today's flag was introduced in 1845. The eight stripes represent the state's eight principal islands (in all there are 122).

Idaho

Population: 1,000,000
State capital: Boise
Population: 110,000
Area: 83,560 sq mi (216,400 km²)
State flower: syringa (mock orange)
State bird: mountain bluebird
State tree: western white pine
Motto: *Esto Perpetua* ("It is Forever")

Idaho was the 43rd State of the Union (3 July 1890). The flag – adopted in 1907 and revised in 1957 – shows the state seal. A shield depicting mountainous terrain with a western white pine is supported by a man in mining gear, representing the state's mineral resources, and a woman bearing a spear and a set of scales, representing justice, liberty and equality. Beneath the shield are cornucopias and a wheatsheaf, to symbolize the state's agricultural fertility; and above it is an elk's head, representing the state's wildlife. The seal's circular frame may carry the words "Great Seal of the State of Idaho", while the scroll beneath has "State of Idaho".

Illinois

Population: 11,535,000
State capital: Springfield
Population: 105,000
Area: 56,400 sq mi (146,100 km²)
State flower: native violet
State bird: cardinal
State tree: oak
Motto: State Sovereignty, National Union

Illinois was the 21st State of the Union (3 December 1818). Adopted in 1915, although without the state's name (added in 1970), the flag shows elements from the state seal: a bald eagle on a rock with a shield bearing the stars and stripes of the 13 original states; on the rock are the dates 1868 and 1818. Laurel leaves beneath the shield represent the great achievements of the people of Illinois; in the background the sun rises over the prairie as a symbol of progress – both that made since statehood and that to be made in the glowing future. The design was the winner of a competition organized by the Daughters of the American Revolution.

Indiana

Population: 5,500,000
State capital: Indianapolis
Population: 710,300
Area: 36,300 sq mi (94,000 km²)
State flower: peony
State bird: cardinal
State tree: tulip tree
Motto: The Crossroads of America

Indiana was the 19th State of the Union (11 December 1816). Flushed with the success of their competition for the flag of Illinois, in 1916 the Daughters of the American Revolution ran another for the sake of Indiana's centenary; the winning design was adopted by the state the following year. Surrounding the torch (representing liberty and enlightenment) are 19 stars, the biggest being the 19th state itself, with the name in an arc above it.

USA – STATES OF THE UNION

Iowa

Population: 2,900,000
State capital: Des Moines
Population: 200,000
Area: 56,300 sq mi (145,800 km^2)
State flower: wild rose
State bird: eastern goldfinch
State tree: oak
Motto: Our Liberties We Prize and Our Rights We Will Maintain

Iowa was the 29th State of the Union (28 December 1846). The Daughters of the American Revolution were responsible for the original design of this flag, which shows the bald eagle from the state seal holding in its beak but in a different configuration | a; curving scroll bearing the state motto. The blue and red were added when the flag was ratified in 1921, so that the colours became those of the French tricolour – commemorating Iowa's past as part of French North America.

Kansas

Population: 2,450,000
State capital: Topeka
Population: 120,000
Area: 82,250 sq mi (213,000 km^2)
State flower: sunflower
State bird: western meadowlark
State tree: cottonwood
Motto: *Ad Astra per Aspera* ("To the Stars through Toils")

Kansas was the 34th State of the Union (29 January 1861). The name on the flag dates from 1963. The state seal – showing a landscape (representing the east, whence most of the settlers came), 34 stars, a ploughman and a log cabin (symbolizing faith in the state's agriculture) – is central; above it the state flower surmounts a wreath that represents the Louisiana Purchase of 1803.

Kentucky

Population: 3,730,000
State capital: Frankfort
Population: 27,500
Area: 40,400 sq mi (104,600 km^2)
State flower: goldenrod
State bird: Kentucky cardinal
State tree: tulip poplar
Motto: United We Stand, Divided We Fall

Kentucky was the 15th State of the Union (1 June 1792). Above the central motif from the state seal, which has the state motto framing a depiction of a statesman and a frontiersman clasping hands, are the words "Commonwealth of Kentucky". The state flower is twined into a wreath beneath.

The Seal of the President of the USA

Louisiana

Population: 4,480,000
State capital: Baton Rouge
Population: 240,000
Area: 48,525 sq mi (125,675 km^2)
State flower: magnolia
State bird: brown pelican
State tree: bald cypress
Motto: Union, Justice and Confidence

Louisiana was the 18th State of the Union (30 April 1812). Ratified in 1912, Louisiana's flag shows a mother brown pelican apparently preening herself as part of the preparation for feeding the three open-beaked offspring at her feet; the design is intended to convey a sense of the state's role as protector of its people and its resources. The state motto is on the scroll beneath.

Maine

Population: 1,165,000
State capital: Augusta
Population: 22,000
Area: 33,215 sq mi (86,025 km^2)
State flower: white pine cone and tassel
State bird: chickadee
State tree: white pine
Motto: *Dirigo* ("I Direct")

Maine was the 23rd State of the Union (15 March 1820). The seal at the centre of the flag, adopted in 1909, shows a shield on which are depicted a white pine and a moose (for forestry and untamed wilderness, respectively). Above the shield are a representation of Polaris and the state motto, which should be read in conjunction with the star to indicate Maine's northerly location. The supporters of the shield are a seaman leaning on an anchor (to represent commerce and fishing) and a farmer (to represent agriculture).

USA – STATES OF THE UNION

U

Maryland

Population: 4,395,000
State capital: Annapolis
Population: 32,500
Area: 10,600 sq mi (27,400 km²)
State flower: black-eyed susan
State bird: Baltimore oriole
State tree: white oak
Motto: *Fatti Maschii, Parole Femine*
("Manly Deeds, Womanly Words")

Maryland was the 7th State of the Union (28 April 1788). The flag was ratified in 1924 and reflects the role of the Baltimore family in the state's past. George Calvert (c1580–1632), 1st Baron Baltimore, returned home from Newfoundland in 1821 to obtain a fresh charter; he died before the process was complete, and his son Cecil (c1605–75) inherited both the barony and the territory, which was named Maryland for Charles I's queen, Henrietta Maria (1609–69). It was Cecil's younger brother, Leonard Calvert (1606–47), who became first Governor of Maryland. On the flag the Calverts are represented by their design in yellow and black. On his mother's side the 1st Baron was a Crossland, and the Crossland's design is shown in the flag's other two quarters.

Massachusetts

Population: 5,825,000
State capital: Boston
Population: 580,000
Area: 8,250 sq mi (21,400 km²)
State flower: mayflower
State bird: chickadee
State tree: American elm
Motto: *Ense Petit Placidam sub Libertate Quietem* ("By the Sword We Seek Peace, but Peace only under Liberty")

Massachusetts was the 6th State of the Union (6 February 1788). In view of the wording of the state motto, which appears on the scroll around the shield, the depiction of an Amerindian armed with a bow might seem inapposite, but in fact he has been a symbol of the state since 1629. The star on the shield signifies membership of the Union. Above the shield is a human arm wielding a sword, in demonstration of the motto. Between 1908 and 1971 the Massachusetts flag had a quite different design on the reverse, showing a similar shield but with a pine tree in place of the Amerindian.

Michigan

Population: 9,100,000
State capital: Lansing
Population: 130,000
Area: 58,220 sq mi (150,800 km²)
State flower: apple blossom
State bird: robin
State tree: white pine
Mottoes: *Si Quaeris Peninsulam Amoenam, Circumspice* ("If You Seek a Pleasant Peninsula, Look Around You") and *Tuebor* ("I Will Defend")

Michigan was the 26th State of the Union (26 January 1837). The longer of the two state mottoes is in the scroll beneath the shield, which comes from the state seal; the shorter motto is on the shield itself; on a scroll above is *E Pluribus Unum*. Supported by an elk and a moose and surmounted by a bald eagle, the shield has features including a rising sun of freedom. The current version of the flag dates from 1911.

Minnesota

Population: 4,200,000
State capital: St Paul
Population: 268,000
Area: 84,000 sq mi (217,750 km²)
State flower: pink and white lady's slipper
State bird: common loon
State tree: Norway pine
Motto: *L'étoile du Nord* ("Star of the North")

Minnesota was the 32nd State of the Union (11 May 1858). Introduced in 1893 and revised in 1957, the flag shows the state seal, with motto. There are 19 stars in the seal's circular white frame to indicate that Minnesota was the 19th State of the Union after the original 13 – perhaps it would have been embarrassing to try to cram in 32 stars. The scene in the seal shows a ploughman (representing agriculture), a tree-stump (lumbering) and an Ameridian (Minnesota's heritage); the version of the seal used on the flag is decorated with the dates 1819, 1858 and 1893, these being, respectively, the years of first settlement, the attainment of statehood and the initial adoption of the flag.

USA – STATES OF THE UNION

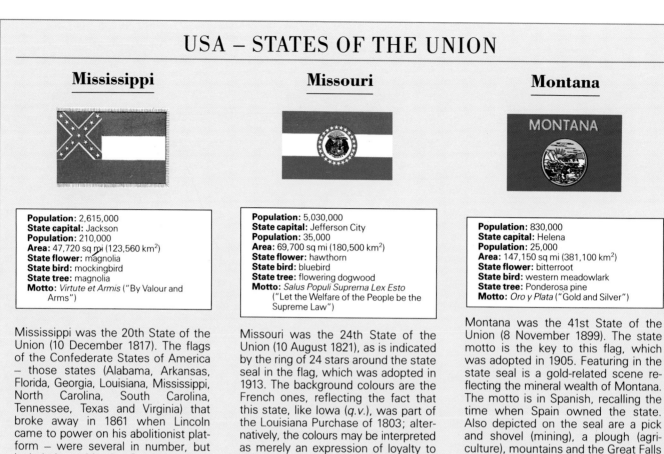

Mississippi

Population: 2,615,000
State capital: Jackson
Population: 210,000
Area: 47,720 sq mi (123,560 km^2)
State flower: magnolia
State bird: mockingbird
State tree: magnolia
Motto: *Virtute et Armis* ("By Valour and Arms")

Missouri

Population: 5,030,000
State capital: Jefferson City
Population: 35,000
Area: 69,700 sq mi (180,500 km^2)
State flower: hawthorn
State bird: bluebird
State tree: flowering dogwood
Motto: *Salus Populi Suprema Lex Esto* ("Let the Welfare of the People be the Supreme Law")

Montana

Population: 830,000
State capital: Helena
Population: 25,000
Area: 147,150 sq mi (381,100 km^2)
State flower: bitterroot
State bird: western meadowlark
State tree: Ponderosa pine
Motto: *Oro y Plata* ("Gold and Silver")

Mississippi was the 20th State of the Union (10 December 1817). The flags of the Confederate States of America – those states (Alabama, Arkansas, Florida, Georgia, Louisiana, Mississippi, North Carolina, South Carolina, Tennessee, Texas and Virginia) that broke away in 1861 when Lincoln came to power on his abolitionist platform – were several in number, but included notably the Stars and Bars and the Battle Flag. The Stars and Bars reflected the Stars and Stripes: in place of the stripes were three horizontal bands, red over white over red; the stars were arranged in a circle in a box at upper left. The square Battle Flag (also known as the Southern Cross) had a red background with a white-edged diagonal blue cross on it, stars being arranged along the arms of the cross. The Mississippi flag combines both designs, although with the upper band from the Stars and Bars in blue rather than red. The flag was adopted in 1894.

Missouri was the 24th State of the Union (10 August 1821), as is indicated by the ring of 24 stars around the state seal in the flag, which was adopted in 1913. The background colours are the French ones, reflecting the fact that this state, like Iowa (*q.v.*), was part of the Louisiana Purchase of 1803; alternatively, the colours may be interpreted as merely an expression of loyalty to the Union. On the seal, two grizzly bears (representing the state's fortitude and its citizens' courage) are beneath a starry sky (again 24 stars); they support a shield on which are depicted the arms of the USA, a crescent moon and a bear.

Montana was the 41st State of the Union (8 November 1899). The state motto is the key to this flag, which was adopted in 1905. Featuring in the state seal is a gold-related scene reflecting the mineral wealth of Montana. The motto is in Spanish, recalling the time when Spain owned the state. Also depicted on the seal are a pick and shovel (mining), a plough (agriculture), mountains and the Great Falls of the Missouri River. Since 1981 the state's name has officially been an integral part of the flag, although it does not always appear.

The "Southern Cross" or "flag of the South"

USA – STATES OF THE UNION

Nebraska

Population: 1,600,000
State capital: Lincoln
Population: 182,000
Area: 77,230 sq mi (200,020 km²)
State flower: goldenrod
State bird: western meadowlark
State tree: American elm
Motto: Equality Before the Law

Nebraska was the 37th State of the Union (1 March 1867). The Daughters of the American Revolution inspired the state to adopt its flag in 1925 (it was revised in 1963). The centre of the design is the state seal. On the seal are a smith with hammer and anvil (industry), wheatsheaves, stalks of growing corn and a settlers' cabin (all denoting agriculture), a Missouri River steamboat and a train (the transportation that has helped speed Nebraska's development) and the Rocky Mountains; above all this the state motto is enscrolled across the sky. Troops from the state had earlier used a version of the flag unofficially during World War I.

Nevada

Population: 940,000
State capital: Carson City
Population: 36,000
Area: 110,550 sq mi (286,300 km²)
State flower: sagebrush
State bird: mountain bluebird
State tree: single-leaf piñon
Mottoes: All for Our Country *and* Battle Born

Nevada was the 36th State of the Union (31 October 1864). It was during the American Civil War that Nevada was admitted to the Union, and this is reflected by use of the motto "Battle Born" in the flag. The star represents the state, and the boughs beneath are

of the state plant, the sagebrush. The flag was adopted in 1929, having been a competition winner in 1926.

New Hampshire

Population: 1,000,000
State capital: Concord
Population: 32,000
Area: 9,300 sq mi (24,100 km²)
State flower: purple lilac
State bird: purple finch
State tree: white birch
Motto: Live Free or Die

New Hampshire was the 9th State of the Union (21 June 1788). Adopted in 1909 (revised 1932), the state flag shows the seal, depicting the building of the frigate *Raleigh* at Portsmouth during the War of American Independence; at the ship's stern flies the US flag of 1777. In the foreground is a granite boulder to symbolize the ruggedness of both the state's terrain and its people's temperament. The surrounding ring of laurel with nine stars has the obvious meaning.

New Jersey

Population: 7,600,000
State capital: Trenton
Population: 93,000
Area: 7,840 sq mi (20,300 km²)
State flower: purple violet
State bird: eastern goldfinch
State tree: red oak
Motto: Liberty and Prosperity

New Jersey was the 3rd State of the Union (18 December 1787). Adopted in 1938, the flag features the shield from the state arms with the state motto on a scroll beneath. One of the supporters – Ceres, the Greek goddess of agri-

culture – contributes to a general agricultural theme that focuses on the three ploughs depicted on the shield; the other supporter is Liberty. Above the shield is the helmet of a ruler (indicating the state's sovereignty) and above that is a horse's head (representing agriculture, again, but also commerce, speed and strength). The buff-coloured background reflects the uniforms worn by the state's military during the War of American Independence.

U

New Mexico

Population: 1,450,000
State capital: Santa Fé
Population: 53,000
Area: 122,000 sq mi (315,115 km²)
State flower: yucca
State bird: roadrunner
State tree: piñon
Motto: *Crescit eundo* ("It Grows as It Goes")

New Mexico was the 47th State of the Union (6 January 1912) and adopted its elegantly simple flag in 1925. The Spanish traditions of the state are obvious in the choice of colours – crimson and gold – and its Indian heritage is also manifest in the symbol of the sun, which is based on an emblem of the Zia Pueblos and signifies harmony between those from different cultures acting in union.

USA – STATES OF THE UNION

New York

Population: 17,800,000
State capital: Albany
Population: 100,000
Area: 49,600 sq mi (128,400 km^2)
State flower: rose
State bird: bluebird
State tree: sugar maple
Motto: *Excelsior* ("Ever Upward")

New York was the 11th State of the Union (26 July 1788). Before 1901 the background colour of its flag was buff rather than blue. The state arms show an eagle above a shield that is supported by two figures representing justice and liberty. On the shield is the sun rising over mountains above the Hudson River, on whose waters are two ships.

North Carolina

Population: 6,300,000
State capital: Raleigh
Population: 172,000
Area: 52,600 sq mi (136,200 km^2)
State flower: flowering dogwood
State bird: cardinal
State tree: pine
Motto: *Esse Quam Videri* ("To Be, Rather than to Seem")

North Carolina was the 12th State of the Union (21 November 1789). Like those of Mississippi (*q.v.*) and several other states, the flag of Missouri reflects the colours of the Confederate States of America. Two scrolls bearing dates appear in the vertical blue stripe.

The upper one, May 20th 1775, is for the Mecklenburg Declaration of Independence, supposedly signed on that day; the lower one, April 12th 1776, is the date on which North Carolina authorized its delegates to vote for independence at the Continental Congress – an intention more forcefully presented a few months later, on 4 July. The historical status of the Mecklenburg Declaration of Independence – whereby a group of citizens supposedly declared Mecklenburg County, NC, independent of the UK – is dubious. In 1819 a group of men claimed that they had attended such a meeting on 20 May, but no written evidence exists for it having taken place. There are, however, records that a meeting took place on the 31st of that month, although its purpose was just a general gripe about the meannesses of the British masters and nothing was decided, so it is possible that memory, 44 years later, misled the claimants as to the date and nature of this gathering. The flag was adopted in 1885.

Skyscrapers tower above Battery Park, at the southern tip of Manhattan, New York City. They face the Statue of Liberty on Liberty Island.

USA – STATES OF THE UNION

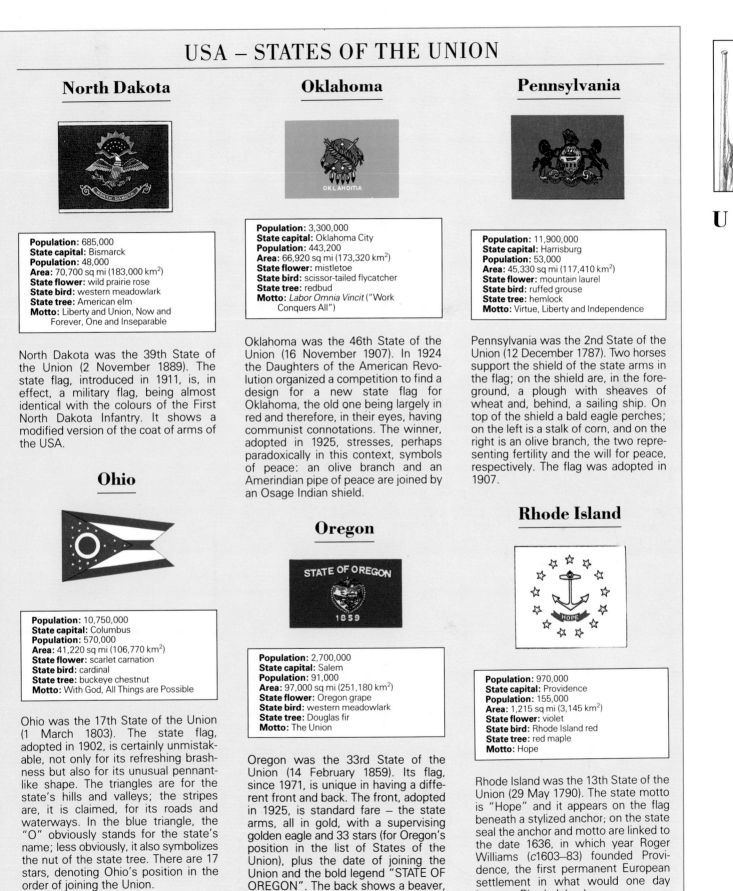

North Dakota

Population: 685,000
State capital: Bismarck
Population: 48,000
Area: 70,700 sq mi (183,000 km²)
State flower: wild prairie rose
State bird: western meadowlark
State tree: American elm
Motto: Liberty and Union, Now and Forever, One and Inseparable

North Dakota was the 39th State of the Union (2 November 1889). The state flag, introduced in 1911, is, in effect, a military flag, being almost identical with the colours of the First North Dakota Infantry. It shows a modified version of the coat of arms of the USA.

Ohio

Population: 10,750,000
State capital: Columbus
Population: 570,000
Area: 41,220 sq mi (106,770 km²)
State flower: scarlet carnation
State bird: cardinal
State tree: buckeye chestnut
Motto: With God, All Things are Possible

Ohio was the 17th State of the Union (1 March 1803). The state flag, adopted in 1902, is certainly unmistakable, not only for its refreshing brashness but also for its unusual pennant-like shape. The triangles are for the state's hills and valleys; the stripes are, it is claimed, for its roads and waterways. In the blue triangle, the "O" obviously stands for the state's name; less obviously, it also symbolizes the nut of the state tree. There are 17 stars, denoting Ohio's position in the order of joining the Union.

Oklahoma

Population: 3,300,000
State capital: Oklahoma City
Population: 443,200
Area: 66,920 sq mi (173,320 km²)
State flower: mistletoe
State bird: scissor-tailed flycatcher
State tree: redbud
Motto: *Labor Omnia Vincit* ("Work Conquers All")

Oklahoma was the 46th State of the Union (16 November 1907). In 1924 the Daughters of the American Revolution organized a competition to find a design for a new state flag for Oklahoma, the old one being largely in red and therefore, in their eyes, having communist connotations. The winner, adopted in 1925, stresses, perhaps paradoxically in this context, symbols of peace: an olive branch and an Amerindian pipe of peace are joined by an Osage Indian shield.

Oregon

Population: 2,700,000
State capital: Salem
Population: 91,000
Area: 97,000 sq mi (251,180 km²)
State flower: Oregon grape
State bird: western meadowlark
State tree: Douglas fir
Motto: The Union

Oregon was the 33rd State of the Union (14 February 1859). Its flag, since 1971, is unique in having a different front and back. The front, adopted in 1925, is standard fare – the state arms, all in gold, with a supervising golden eagle and 33 stars (for Oregon's position in the list of States of the Union), plus the date of joining the Union and the bold legend "STATE OF OREGON". The back shows a beaver, to reflect the old fur trade.

Pennsylvania

Population: 11,900,000
State capital: Harrisburg
Population: 53,000
Area: 45,330 sq mi (117,410 km²)
State flower: mountain laurel
State bird: ruffed grouse
State tree: hemlock
Motto: Virtue, Liberty and Independence

Pennsylvania was the 2nd State of the Union (12 December 1787). Two horses support the shield of the state arms in the flag; on the shield are, in the foreground, a plough with sheaves of wheat and, behind, a sailing ship. On top of the shield a bald eagle perches; on the left is a stalk of corn, and on the right is an olive branch, the two representing fertility and the will for peace, respectively. The flag was adopted in 1907.

Rhode Island

Population: 970,000
State capital: Providence
Population: 155,000
Area: 1,215 sq mi (3,145 km²)
State flower: violet
State bird: Rhode Island red
State tree: red maple
Motto: Hope

Rhode Island was the 13th State of the Union (29 May 1790). The state motto is "Hope" and it appears on the flag beneath a stylized anchor; on the state seal the anchor and motto are linked to the date 1636, in which year Roger Williams (c1603–83) founded Providence, the first permanent European settlement in what would one day become Rhode Island.

U

97

USA – STATES OF THE UNION

South Carolina

Population: 3,350,000
State capital: Columbia
Population: 99,000
Area: 31,050 sq mi (80,430 km²)
State flower: Carolina jessamine
State bird: Carolina wren
State tree: palmetto
Mottoes: *Animis Opibusque Parati* ("Prepared in Mind and Resources") and *Dum Spiro Spero* ("While I Breathe, I Hope")

South Carolina was the 8th State of the Union (23 May 1788). Adopted in 1861, the flag has a certain nightclub feel to it, but the two images are in fact of venerable origin. The central palmetto is the state tree, and was used as an emblem during the American Civil War. It is drawn from the state seal, which shows a palmetto surmounting a dead oak tree, a visual record of how in 1776 during the War of American Independence the palmetto-log fort of Sullivan's Island, SC, was successfully defended against the oak ships of the British. The crescent likewise dates back to the War of American Independence, when in 1775 the troops began to wear a cap badge featuring both the crescent and the motto "Liberty or Death"

South Dakota

Population: 710,000
State capital: Pierre
Population: 12,500
Area: 77,050 sq mi (199,560 km²)
State flower: pasqueflower
State bird: ring-necked pheasant
State tree: Black Hills spruce
Motto: Under God the People Rule

South Dakota was the 40th State of the Union (2 November 1889). The state's original flag, adopted in 1909, showed on the front a brilliantly blazing sun on a blue background, with the words "South Dakota The Sunshine State" around it. On the reverse was the state seal. Since 1963 the official design has been one-sided, the seal obliterating all but the fringes of the sun. On the seal is a landscape laden with symbolism. Grazing cattle represent ranching and dairying, and a ploughing farmer and a field of corn denote agriculture, while the state's mining industry is commemorated by a smelting furnace. In the background is a steamboat on the Missouri River to symbolize transportation and commerce.

Tennessee

Population: 4,765,000
State capital: Nashville
Population: 465,000
Area: 42,250 sq mi (109,410 km²)
State flower: iris
State bird: mockingbird
State tree: tulip poplar
Motto: Agriculture and Commerce

Tennessee was the 16th State of the Union (1 June 1796). The meaning of the three stars in the centre of the flag, adopted in 1905, is dubious; one explanation would seem to be that they indicate that Tennessee was the third state to join the Union after the original 13; an alternative proposition is that they represent East, Middle and West Tennessee. The colours are those of the Confederate States of America.

Texas

Population: 16,375,000
State capital: Austin
Population: 400,000
Area: 267,340 sq mi (692,410 km²)
State flower: bluebonnet
State bird: mockingbird
State tree: pecan
Motto: Friendship

Texas was the 28th State of the Union (29 December 1845). The original Texan flag, adopted in 1819, long before Texas joined the Union, had a prominent single star on a blue background – hence Texas's nickname, the "Lone Star State". The red is here interpreted to mean bravery, the white purity and the blue loyalty. The current design was adopted in 1839.

Utah

Population: 1,650,000
State capital: Salt Lake City
Population: 165,000
Area: 85,000 sq mi (220,000 km²)
State flower: sego lily
State bird: seagull
State tree: blue spruce
Motto: Industry

Utah was the 45th State of the Union (4 January 1896). The beehive in the centre of Utah's state seal – representing hard work and industry (a meaning stressed by the appearance of the word "Industry" above the image) – is a sign of the Mormons, and hence a reminder that before the United States acquired the territory in 1850 it was briefly the Mormon Deseret; the date 1847, which appears on the flag, is the year in which the Mormons first came to settle here. The bald eagle and the flags are US national symbols, affirming the state's loyalty. When the flag was adopted in 1913 the initial manufacturer had whimsically added a gold circle around the seal. In a reversal of normal bureaucratic decision-making, this unauthorized embellishment, even though widely regarded as an improvement, was adopted as part of the official flag.

USA – STATES OF THE UNION

U

Vermont

Population: 540,000
State capital: Montpelier
Population: 8,500
Area: 9,610 sq mi (24,900 km²)
State flower: red clover
State bird: hermit thrush
State trees: sugar maple, pine
Motto: Freedom and Unity

Vermont was the 14th State of the Union (4 March 1791). The flag, adopted in 1923, has uncertain origins, although it seems that something like it had been used by the Vermont military. The tree at the centre of the shield is a pine; behind it is a backdrop of mountains and beside it are a cow and three wheatsheaves to represent the state's agriculture. The central portion of the scroll beneath bears the state's name; the two sections at the sides carry the motto.

Virginia

Population: 5,710,000
State capital: Richmond
Population: 220,000
Area: 40,820 sq mi (105,720 km²)
State flower: flowering dogwood
State bird: cardinal
Motto: *Sic Semper Tyrannis* ("Thus Always to Tyrants")

Virginia was the 10th State of the Union (25 June 1788). Adopted in this form in 1931, the flag shows the version of the state seal adopted in 1776; the original version of the flag dates from 1761 – i.e., it predates Virginia's attainment of statehood. The seal shows the figure of Virtue, dressed as an Amazon and holding a spear and a re-sheathed sword, standing triumphant over the corpse of a slain tyrant (hence the relevance of the motto), who is still clutching a broken length of chain and whose crown is lying lost on the ground nearby. In 1861, of course, the "tyrant" concerned was Abraham Lincoln (Virginia was one of the states seceding to form the Confederate States of America in response to Lincoln's abolitionist promises), so it is perhaps surprising that the flag was not modified before adoption.

Washington

Population: 4,410,000
State capital: Olympia
Population: 30,000
Area: 68,200 sq mi (176,620 km²)
State flower: coast rhododendron
State bird: willow goldfinch
State tree: western hemlock
Motto: *Alki* ("Bye and Bye")

Washington was the 42nd State of the Union (11 November 1889). The state's nickname is the "Evergreen State", and so it is fitting its flag should have a green (for forestry) background. Adopted in 1923 although introduced as early as 1915, the flag includes the state seal, depicting Washington himself. Initially the seal used a postage stamp for the image of Washington, but in 1967 a portrait by the US artist Gilbert Stuart (1755–1828) was adopted in its place for both seal and flag.

West Virginia

Population: 1,950,000
State capital: Charleston
Population: 68,000
Area: 24,180 sq mi (62,630 km²)
State flower: rhododendron
State bird: cardinal
State tree: sugar maple
Motto: *Montani Semper Liberi* ("Mountain Men are Always Free")

West Virginia was the 35th State of the Union (20 June 1863). The meaning of the state's motto may seem rather opaque – especially when translated, as it sometimes is, as "Mountaineers are Always Free" – until you realize that it was coined at the subdivision of the old Virginia at the time of the American Civil War, the current West Virginia refusing to follow the rest of the state into secession. The shield, from the state seal, is framed by rhododendron flowers and leaves. On it are depicted a miner and a farmer with, between them, a rock on which appears the date 1863, denoting West Virginia's attainment of statehood. Rifles are placed in the foreground as a sign of the willingness of the state's citizens to do battle for their freedom. The current version of the flag was adopted in 1929.

The Supreme Court, in Washington DC is the highest court in the judiciary. Under the federal system of government, each state is self governing in local matters, with its own executive (the Governor), legislature and judiciary.

Wisconsin

Population: 4,780,000
State capital: Madison
Population: 172,000
Area: 56,150 sq mi (145,440 km²)
State flower: wood violet
State bird: robin
State tree: sugar maple
Motto: Forward

Wisconsin was the 30th State of the Union (29 May 1848). There is a hiccup in the history of the state's flag, in that in 1887 a legal foul-up resulted in its being officially abolished; it was not reinstated (in a somewhat revised version) until 1929. The flag was further revised in 1981 by the addition of the name and of the year in which Wisconsin joined the Union. The main feature of the flag is the state seal, adopted in 1881. It depicts a miner and a seaman supporting a shield on which appear symbols of navigation, mining, transportation and agriculture as well as a US coat of arms affirming the state's loyalty to the Union. Above the shield is a badger, reflecting the fact that Wisconsin's nickname is the Badger State.

Wyoming

Population: 510,000
State capital: Cheyenne
Population: 52,000
Area: 97,915 sq mi (253,600 km²)
State flower: Indian paintbrush
State bird: meadowlark
State tree: cottonwood
Motto: Equal Rights

Wyoming was the 44th State of the Union (10 July 1890). The state flag was adopted in 1917, the design having won a competition organized by the Daughters of the American Revolution the year before. In fact, the design has since been revised several times to produce the modern version, which has the buffalo facing the pole and the state seal superimposed on the buffalo, in conscious imitation of the branding of livestock. Wyoming was the first of all the states to grant unrestricted civil and political rights to women (1869), and this is acknowledged on the seal both by the motto and by the appearance of the figure of a woman. The state's ranching and mining industries are represented on the seal by the figures of a cowboy and a miner. The red of the flag's border represents the blood of the pioneers and the colour of the skins of the territory's aboriginal inhabitants.

District of Columbia

Population: 3,430,000
Population of City of Washington: 623,000
Area: 69 sq mi (179 km²)

Although not itself a state, the District of Columbia has a flag whose origins can be traced back further than those of any state with the possible exception of Maryland. Introduced in 1938, the flag has the arms of George Washington, granted to his ancestors, the Washingtons of Sulgrave Manor, Northamptonshire, England, in 1592.

U

USA – ASSOCIATED LANDS

American Samoa

Population: 37,000
Capital: Pago Pago
Population: 2,500
Area: 77 sq mi (197 km^2)
Economy: coconuts, copra, fishing, bananas, cocoa, canned fish

The eastern part of Samoa (see also Western Samoa) has belonged to the United States since 1899, but has been a self-governing dependency since 1960, when this flag was adopted. US symbolism proliferates – both in the colours (although these can be regarded as being also from Samoan tradition) and in the presence of the bald eagle. In its talons the eagle has two symbols of Samoan authority, a chief's war-club and whisk or ritual staff.

Guam

Population: 126,000
Capital: Agaña
Population: 2,200
Area: 215 sq mi (550 km^2)
Economy: agriculture, fruit, sugar, fishing

The flag of Guam, designed by a naval officer's wife and adopted in 1917, can be flown only in conjunction with the US flag. Adapted from the seal, the scene shows a palm tree and a boat as well as a stylized version of the Agaña River's estuary. The flag's red border was added in 1960.

Midway Island

Population: 600
Administrative centre: Midway
Population: 470
Area: 3 sq mi (8 km^2)
Economy: naval base

A US possession since 1867, Midway is an atoll containing two islands and is about 1,150 miles (1,850 km) northwest of Honolulu. It uses the US flag.

Virgin Islands of the United States

Population: 107,000
Capital: Charlotte Amalie
Population: 11,700
Area: 135 sq mi (345 km^2)
Economy: tourism, rum, oil and bauxite processing, watches, pharmaceuticals

Designed by a sailor and adopted in 1921, the flag is based on the US coat of arms. The bald eagle, in yellow, clutches three blue arrows with one foot and an olive branch with the other. The flag is for use on land only.

Wake Island

Population: 1,650
Administrative centre: Wake
Area: 3 sq mi (8 km^2)
Economy: naval base

This territory has only an unofficial flag. It colours are red for courage, yellow for loyalty, white for truth and blue for the ocean. Despite its name, the territory in fact comprises three islands – Peale, Wake and Wilkes, Wake being the biggest – and these are shown in the flag's map.

UPPER VOLTA

See Burkina Faso

URUGUAY

Oriental Republic of
República Oriental del Uruguay

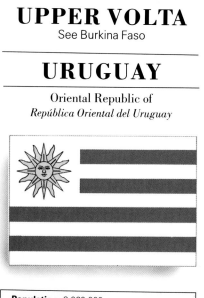

Population: 3,060,000
Capital: Montevideo
Population: 1,330,000
Area: 68,500 sq mi (177,500 km²)
Currency: 100 centésimos = 1 new peso
Language: Spanish
Religion: Christianity (mainly RC)
Economy: agriculture, meat, leather, gems, oil refining, fishing, tourism

In 1828, on gaining independence (with UK and Argentine help) not only from its traditional Spanish overlords but also from Brazil, which had opportunistically invaded in 1820, Uruguay wished to use for its flag the same liberation colours as Argentina (*q.v.*) as well as the revolutionary symbol of the Sun of May. The model chosen for the new flag was the Stars and Stripes of the United States of America (*q.v.*), which had gained its own independence only some 50 years earlier. The nine alternate stripes of blue and white represent the nine original departments of Uruguay. The flag of 1828 was adapted into its current form in 1830; since then the details of the solar image have from time to time been revised.

UZBEKISTAN

Ozbekistan

Population: 17,990,000
Capital: Taskent (Tashkent)
Population: 1,985,000
Area: 172,800 sq mi (447,600 km²)
Languages: Turkic languages
Religion: Islam
Economy: cotton, fruit, silk, rice, wheat, corn, grapes, sheep, coal, oil, gas, copper, chemicals, agricultural machinery, textiles, paper

Uzbekistan has been a unitary state since 1991, having become so at the time of the general dissolution of the Union of Soviet Socialist Republics. It gained its name from Khan Uzbek (1312–42), one of the Golden Horde of Tatar warriors that terrorized and conquered much of Asia and eastern Europe during the 13th century. Earlier the region had been invaded by Persians under Darius I (*c*558–486BC), the Macedonians under Alexander the Great (356–323BC) and, in the 7th–8th centuries, the Arabs. By the 16th century the Uzbek people had come to dominate the region, and in the late 19th century Uzbekistan became Russian; in 1924 it was established as the Uzbek SSR.

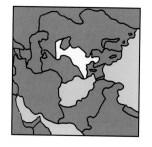

VANUATU

Republic of
Ripablik blong Vanuatu

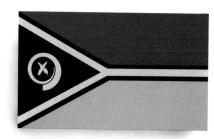

Population: 150,000
Capital: Port-Vila
Population: 15,000
Area: 5,700 sq mi (14,760 km²)
Currency: vatu
Languages: Pidgin English, French, indigenous languages
Religions: Christianity (mainly Protestant), indigenous religions
Economy: copra, cocoa, coffee, beef, tourism, fishing, manganese

On a map the islands that form Vanuatu form a rough Y, and this shape is overt in the flag adopted a few months before the republic gained its independence in 1980. Within the angle of the Y is a boar's tusk, a native emblem of plenty; within the tusk are two leaves of a local fern (*namele*), which symbolizes peace; their 39 fronds represent the 39 members of the nation's legislative assembly.

VATICAN CITY

State of the
Stato della Città del Vaticano

Population: 770
Area: 0.17 sq mi (0.44 km²)
Currency: 100 centesimi = 1 lira (Vatican City)
Languages: Latin, Italian
Religion: Christianity (RC)

The Vatican City State was created in 1929, and the flag it adopted then has remained unchanged. Based on a merchant flag used by the Papal States from 1825 until they were absorbed into the unified Italy in 1870, it shows, beneath the papal triple crown, an image of the keys referred to in *Matthew, xvi,* 18–19: "And I say also unto thee, That thou art Peter, and upon this rock I will build my church . . . And I will give unto thee the keys of the kingdom of heaven: and whatsoever thou shalt bind on earth shalt be bound in heaven: and whatsoever thou shalt loose on earth shall be loosed in heaven." One key is in gold and the other in silver, these two colours representing, respectively, binding and loosing; the red cord tying the keys shows that these powers operate together. The yellow and white of the background reflect the colours of the keys.

VENEZUELA

Republic of
República de Venezuela

Population: 18,750,000
Capital: Caracas
Population: 4,100,000
Area: 352,000 sq mi (912,000 km²)
Currency: 100 céntimos = 1 bolivar
Language: Spanish
Religion: Christianity (almost exclusively RC)
Economy: agriculture, oil, meat, coffee, cocoa, metals, diamonds, coal

The reasons for the similarities between the flag of Venezuela and those of Ecuador and Colombia (*qq.v.*) are discussed in the text accompanying the Colombian flag. The yellow, blue and red colours of all three were those adopted by the Venezuelan freedom fighter Francisco de Miranda (1750–1816) – he fought in the American Revolutionary War and the French Revolution as well as in the Spanish-American Revolution – to convey the message that the nation (yellow) was separated by the sea (blue) from Spain, the red seemingly indicating both the liberation of the South American territories and the blood their people were willing to shed in attaining that freedom. The current version of the Venezuelan flag was adopted in 1954. The seven stars in the central stripe represent the seven provinces of Venezuela liberated by de Miranda in 1811; they appeared in different arrangements in earlier versions of the flag. The complicated national arms – white horse, wheat-sheaf, battle-colours, etc – have a likewise complicated scroll beneath them whose legend has varied according to the political climes.

V

ABOVE **The Venezuelan flag is waved enthusiastically at a May Day parade in the capital, Caracas.**

VIETNAM

Socialist Republic of
Công Hòa Xã Hôi Chu Nghìa Viêt Nam

Population: 64,200,000
Capital: Hanoi
Population: 2,572,000
Area: 127,000 sq mi (330,000 km²)
Currency: 100 xu = 1 dong
Languages: Vietnamese, Chinese, French, English
Religion: Buddhism (Christian minority)
Economy: agriculture, rice, coal, metals, clothing, rubber, tea, coffee

A form of the modern Vietnamese flag was used by the soldiers of Ho Chi Minh (1892–1969) in their struggle against the Japanese during World War II. The Japanese expelled, the struggle of Ho Chi Minh's freedom fighters was now directed against the colonial French; his communist troops continued to fly the red flag with a rather stubby-pointed yellow star, which had the usual socialist meanings. In 1954 the French were ousted, and the Geneva Conference established the communist North Vietnam and the supposedly democratic South Vietnam. The North continued to use Ho Chi Minh's flag, revising it slightly in 1955, utilizing a more orthodox version of the communist star. Civil war between the two states continued until 1975, when the North subsumed the South (which had been aided by the USA since 1961), declaring a reunited socialist republic and adopting the 1955 flag for the whole country.

VIRGIN ISLANDS

See United Kingdom *and* United States of America

WAKE ISLAND

See United States of America

WALLIS AND FUTUNA ISLANDS

See France

WESTERN SAHARA

Population: 175,000
Capital: Laâyoune (El Aiun)
Population: 30,000
Area: 103,000 sq mi (267,000 km²)
Currency: 100 centimes = 1 dirham (Moroccan)
Languages: Arabic, Berber, Spanish
Religion: Islam
Economy: phosphates, fishing, iron

Western Sahara is currently a nation under occupation. Colonized by Spain in 1884 and made a Spanish province in 1960, the country, spearheaded by the Polisario Front, demanded independence in 1973. Before such demands could make headway, however, Morocco in 1975 sent in a vast but weaponless army of invasion. In 1976 the Polisario Front declared the nation – which it called the Saharan Arab Democratic Republic – independent and started a war of liberation. Its flag is in the Pan-Arab colours arranged rather as in the flag of Jordan (*q.v.*), and with a red crescent and star in the white band. Mauritania withdrew in 1979, but Morocco still occupies the country.

WESTERN SAMOA

Independent State of Samoa
Mālōtuto'atasi o Samoa

Population: 167,000
Capital: Apia
Population: 33,200
Area: 1,100 sq mi (2,840 km²)
Currency: 100 sene = 1 tala
Languages: Samoan, English
Religion: Christianity
Economy: copra, coconuts, bananas, cocoa, taro, fishing, tourism

Independence came to Western Samoa in 1962 for the second time; the first had been in 1889, under King Malietoa Laupepa. When he died in 1898, the islands came under the control of Germany, with UK and US agreement. Following World War I New Zealand annexed the islands in 1919, administering them until the second independence, although they were self-governing from 1959. The New Zealand influence is evident in the use of the Southern Cross in the Western Samoan flag, which was established with four stars (as in the New Zealand flag) in 1948 and revised to its modern form, with the additional smaller star, in 1949. The red comes from King Malietoa Laupepa's flag, and the blue from the New Zealand flag.

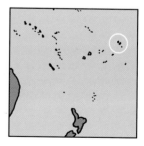

YEMEN

Arab Republic
al-Jamhuriya al-Yamaniya

Population: 11,110,000
Capital: San'a
Population: 440,000
Area: 207,400 sq mi (531,900 km²)
Currency: 100 fils = 1 rial (Yemeni)
Languages: Arabic, English
Religion: Islam
Economy: agriculture, coffee, handicrafts, qat, cotton, oil, sugar, fishing, textiles

Until 22 May 1990 there were two Yemens, North Yemen (or the Yemen Arab Republic) and the larger although less populous South Yemen (or the People's Democratic Republic of Yemen); the modern nation is dominated by the former, as reflected in the national flag. Until 1990 this had been in the Pan-Arab colours shared by Jordan (*q.v.*) and others, but arranged as in that of Syria (*q.v.*), with whom Egypt and North Yemen had formed the United Arab Republic between 1958 and 1961; the North Yemeni flag had a single, five-pointed green star (representing Arab unity) in the central white band. The South Yemeni flag had been essentially a similar tricolour but without the green star and with the superimposition at left of a blue triangle containing a red, nationalist five-pointed star. Today's flag is the simple tricolour.

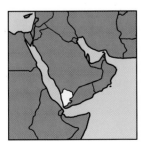

YUGOSLAVIA

Socialist Federal Republic of
Jugoslavia, Jugoslavija

Population: 17,106,700
Capital: Belgrade (Beograd)
Population: 1,150,000
Area: 99,000 sq mi (256,000 km²)
Currency: 100 paras = 1 dinar (Yugoslavian)
Languages: Serbo-Croat, Macedonian, Albanian, others
Religions: Christianity, Islam
Economy: agriculture, fertilizers, animal husbandry, wine, sugar, forestry, fishing, coal, minerals, hydroelectricity, metals, manufacturing, tourism

Until 1991 Yugoslavia contained as republics what have now become the two independent nations of Croatia and Slovenia (*qq.v.*); at the time of writing (March 1992) it seemed possible that Bosnia-Herzegovina would follow in the wake of those two, but not without the period of vicious civil war that had characterized their attainment of independence. Currently, however, there still remain within Yugoslavia four constituent republics, details of which are given in the table. Yugoslavia's history is short. It was formed — "synthesized" might be a better word — in 1918, at the end of World War I (started by an assassin's bullet in 1914 in the city of Sarajevo, capital of Bosnia-Herzegovina), by the federation of Bosnia-Herzegovina, Croatia, Macedonia, Montenegro, Serbia and Slovenia, gaining its modern name in 1927. The country became a monarchy — its King Alexander I (Karageorgovich, 1888–1934) assuming dictatorial powers from 1929 until his assassination in 1934 — and remained so until invaded by Germany in 1941; after freedom came in 1944, Marshal Tito (real name Josip Broz, 1892–1980), who had led one of the two main resistance groups, introduced communism, and it is fair to say that it was the strength of his character which held Yugoslavia together as an independent nation — notably nonaligned with the Soviet bloc, despite (indeed, largely because of) a blockade mounted by that bloc 1948–55 in an effort to bring his regime to its knees. After his death, however, nationalist grumblings rose in volume, with the role of the Croatians during World War II a particular bone of discontent, and it was surprising that his heirs were able to maintain the unity as long as they did. The communist star at the centre of the flag was adopted in 1946; the coloured stripes, representing pan-Slav unity, date from the country's formation in 1918.

Y

CONSTITUENT REPUBLICS WITHIN YUGOSLAVIA

Name	Population	Capital
Bosnia-Herzegovina	4,124,250	Sarajevo
Macedonia	1,910,000	Skopje
Montenegro	584,300	Titograd
Serbia	9,313,700	Belgrade

ZAIRE

Republic of
République du Zaïre

Population: 34,000,000
Capital: Kinshasa
Population: 2,685,000
Area: 905,600 sq mi (2,345,500 km²)
Currency: 100 makuta = 1 zaïre
Languages: French, Lingala, Swahili, Kikongo, Tshiluba
Religions: indigenous religions, Christianity (Islamic minority)
Economy: agriculture, coffee, cotton, palm oil, rubber, copper, diamonds, cobalt, oil, hydroelectricity

Formerly the Belgian Congo, Zaïre has not enjoyed a tranquil history since attaining independence in 1960. Established at first as the Republic of the Congo, it suffered anarchy within days. In 1961 its prime minister, Patrice Lumumba (1925–61), was deposed by his president, Joseph Kasavubu (c1917–69), and the ever more powerful Joseph Désiré Mobutu (1930–); then, in 1965, Mobutu in turn deposed Kasavubu, and he has ruled over a virtual dictatorship ever since. In 1971 Mobutu declared the country a one-party state, with himself as leader of this one party, the MPR (*Mouvement Populaire de la Révolution*) and hence automatically national president; the name of the nation was changed to Zaïre, and a new national flag – almost identical with that of the MPR – introduced. The flag is in the Pan-African red, yellow and green, with their usual meanings; the torch represents liberty and the struggle for it.

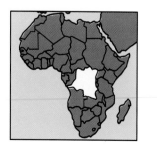

ZAMBIA

Republic of

Population: 7,530,000
Capital: Lusaka
Population: 540,000
Area: 291,000 sq mi (753,000 km²)
Currency: 100 ngwee = 1 kwacha
Languages: English, Bemba, Nyanja and many others
Religions: Christianity, indigenous religions
Economy: mining, copper, and other metals, agriculture, maize, tobacco, peanuts, cotton, sugar, animal husbandry, forestry

When Zambia attained independence in 1964 its first ruling party was the United National Independence Party, led by Kenneth Kaunda (1924–), and this circumstance has obtained ever since, the UNIP being legally confirmed as the country's sole political party in 1972. The colours of the Zambian flag are those that the UNIP claimed for its own in 1964, and the flag has remained unchanged since then even though those of the UNIP have altered. The green background is for the country's agriculture and forestry, the black for its people and the red for the usual progressive sentiments; the curious orangey colour of the third strip reflects the importance of copper in the nation's economy. The eagle signifies the desire for freedom.

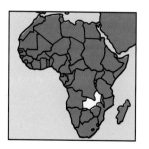

ZIMBABWE

Republic of

Population: 8,900,000
Capital: Harare
Population: 656,000
Area: 151,000 sq mi (391,000 km²)
Currency: 100 cents = 1 dollar (Zimbabwean)
Languages: English, Shona, Ndebele
Religions: Christianity, indigenous religions (Islamic minority)
Economy: agriculture, cotton, tobacco, animal husbandry, fruit, tea, sugar, forestry, fishing, minerals, engineering, textiles, asbestos

The current flag of Zimbabwe was introduced with the declaration of the new republic in 1980, the black central stripe (reflecting the colour of the country's majority) and the Pan-African colours being taken straight from the flag of ZANU (Zimbabwe African National Union), which had been the majority grouping among the forces struggling for majority rule. The black-rimmed white triangle was introduced to symbolize the country's new black rulers' desire for cooperation and peace with the white minority – a laudable generosity · of spirit in view of the nation's history. The five-pointed red star stands for internationalism. The soapstone bird is an emblem associated with the ancient ruined city of Zimbabwe, from which the republic drew its name.

North America

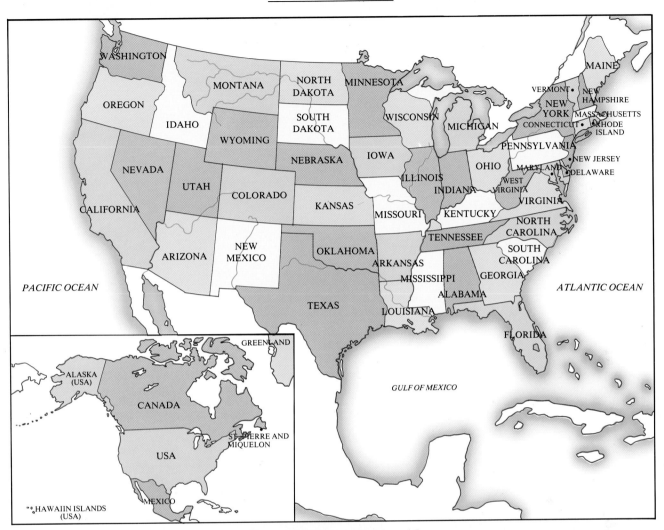

WASHINGTON

MONTANA

NORTH DAKOTA

MINNESOTA

MAINE

OREGON

IDAHO

SOUTH DAKOTA

WISCONSIN

MICHIGAN

VERMONT
NEW HAMPSHIRE
NEW YORK
MASSACHUSETTS
CONNECTICUT
RHODE ISLAND

WYOMING

NEBRASKA

IOWA

PENNSYLVANIA

NEVADA

UTAH

COLORADO

ILLINOIS

INDIANA

OHIO

MARYLAND
NEW JERSEY
DELAWARE

WEST VIRGINIA

CALIFORNIA

KANSAS

MISSOURI

KENTUCKY

VIRGINIA

NORTH CAROLINA

ARIZONA

NEW MEXICO

OKLAHOMA

ARKANSAS

TENNESSEE

SOUTH CAROLINA

PACIFIC OCEAN

MISSISSIPPI

GEORGIA

ALABAMA

ATLANTIC OCEAN

TEXAS

LOUISIANA

FLORIDA

GULF OF MEXICO

GREENLAND

ALASKA (USA)

CANADA

ST. PIERRE AND MIQUELON

USA

MEXICO

HAWAIIN ISLANDS (USA)

Z

Central America and West Indies

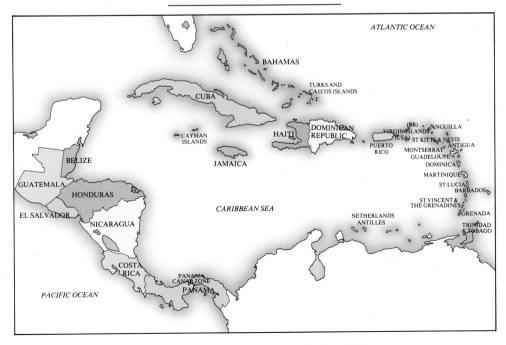

ATLANTIC OCEAN

BAHAMAS

CUBA

TURKS AND CAICOS ISLANDS

CAYMAN ISLANDS

HAITI

DOMINICAN REPUBLIC

(BR) VIRGIN ISLANDS (USA)

ANGUILLA

ST KITTS & NEVIS

PUERTO RICO

MONTSERRAT

ANTIGUA

JAMAICA

GUADELOUPE

DOMINICA

MARTINIQUE

BELIZE

ST LUCIA

BARBADOS

GUATEMALA

HONDURAS

ST VINCENT & THE GRENADINES

GRENADA

EL SALVADOR

NICARAGUA

CARIBBEAN SEA

NETHERLANDS ANTILLES

TRINIDAD & TOBAGO

COSTA RICA

PANAMA CANAL ZONE

PANAMA

PACIFIC OCEAN

107

South America

VENEZUELA

GUYANA

SURINAM

FRENCH GUIANA

COLOMBIA

ECUADOR

PERU

BRAZIL

BOLIVIA

PACIFIC OCEAN

PARAGUAY

CHILE

ARGENTINA

URAGUAY

ATLANTIC OCEAN

FALKLAND ISLANDS

Africa

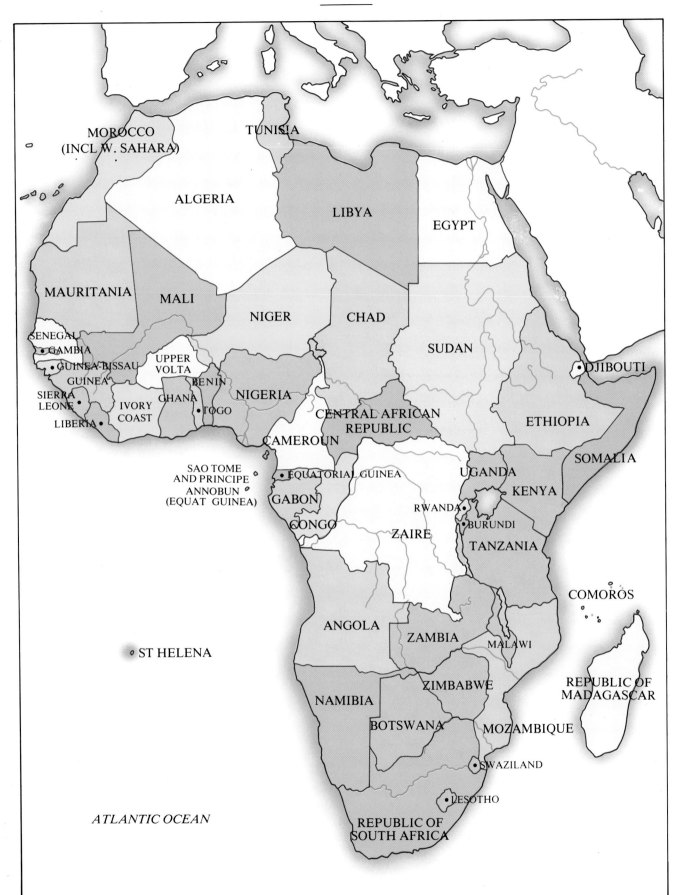

MOROCCO
(INCL W. SAHARA)

TUNISIA

ALGERIA

LIBYA

EGYPT

MAURITANIA

MALI

NIGER

CHAD

SUDAN

SENEGAL

GAMBIA

GUINEA-BISSAU

GUINEA

UPPER
VOLTA

BENIN

NIGERIA

DJIBOUTI

SIERRA
LEONE

GHANA

IVORY
COAST

TOGO

CENTRAL AFRICAN
REPUBLIC

ETHIOPIA

LIBERIA

SAO TOME
AND PRINCIPE
ANNOBUN
(EQUAT GUINEA)

CAMEROUN

EQUATORIAL GUINEA

SOMALIA

GABON

UGANDA

KENYA

CONGO

ZAIRE

RWANDA

BURUNDI

TANZANIA

COMOROS

ANGOLA

ZAMBIA

MALAWI

ST HELENA

ZIMBABWE

REPUBLIC OF
MADAGASCAR

NAMIBIA

BOTSWANA

MOZAMBIQUE

SWAZILAND

LESOTHO

ATLANTIC OCEAN

REPUBLIC OF
SOUTH AFRICA

109

Europe

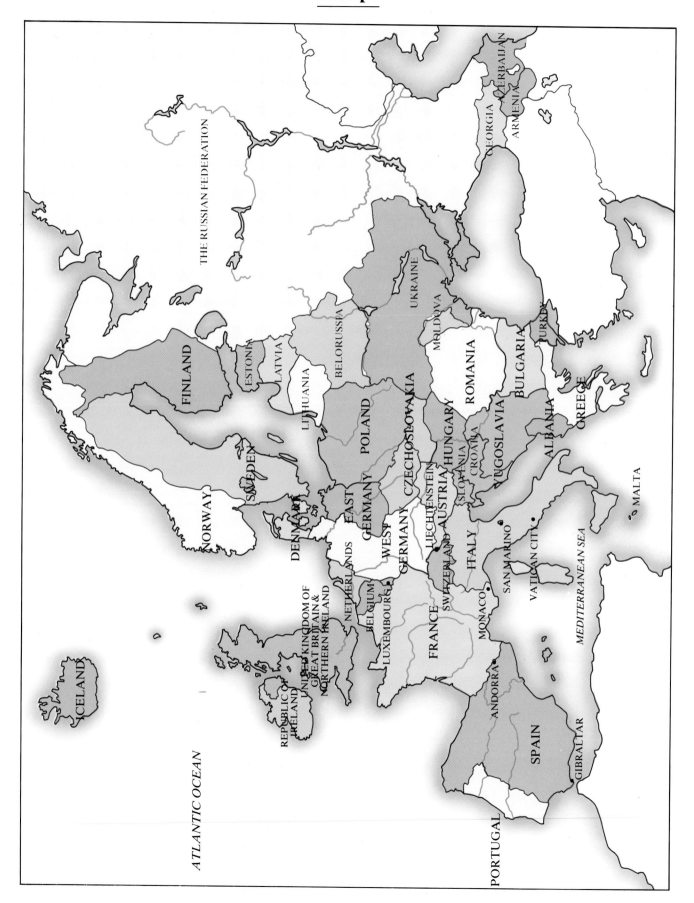

THE RUSSIAN FEDERATION

FINLAND

UKRAINE

ESTONIA

LATVIA

BELORUSSIA

LITHUANIA

POLAND

MOLDOVA

ROMANIA

BULGARIA

TURKEY

GEORGIA

AZERBAIJAN

ARMENIA

SWEDEN

NORWAY

DENMARK

EAST GERMANY

WEST GERMANY

CZECHOSLOVAKIA

AUSTRIA

HUNGARY

LIECHTENSTEIN

SLOVENIA

CROATIA

YUGOSLAVIA

ALBANIA

GREECE

MALTA

NETHERLANDS

BELGIUM

LUXEMBOURG

SWITZERLAND

ITALY

SAN MARINO

VATICAN CITY

MEDITERRANEAN SEA

UNITED KINGDOM OF GREAT BRITAIN & NORTHERN IRELAND

REPUBLIC OF IRELAND

ICELAND

FRANCE

MONACO

ANDORRA

SPAIN

GIBRALTAR

PORTUGAL

ATLANTIC OCEAN

110

Eurasia

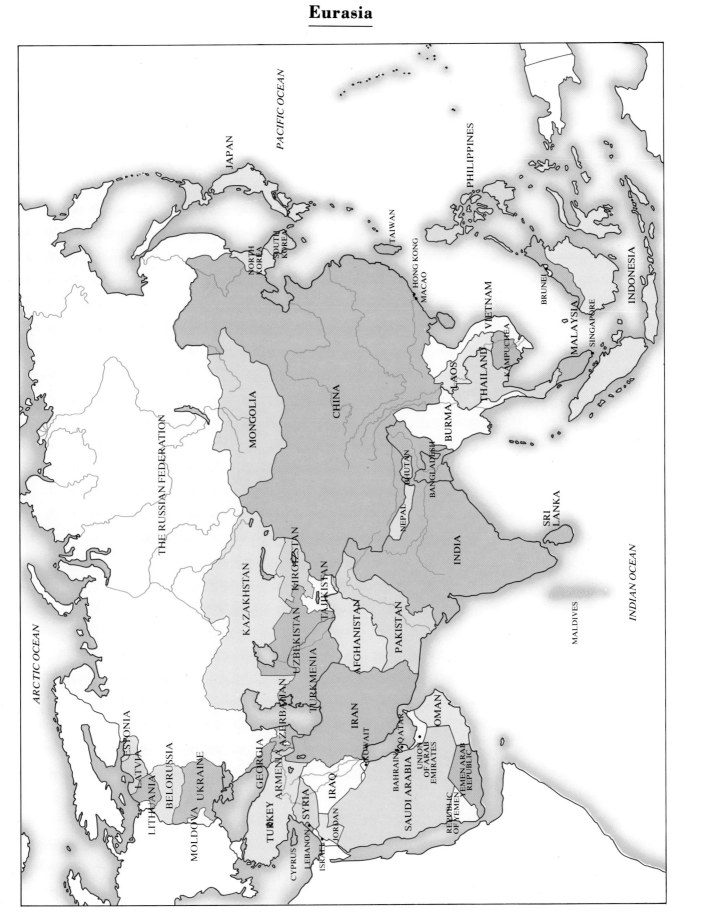

Australasia

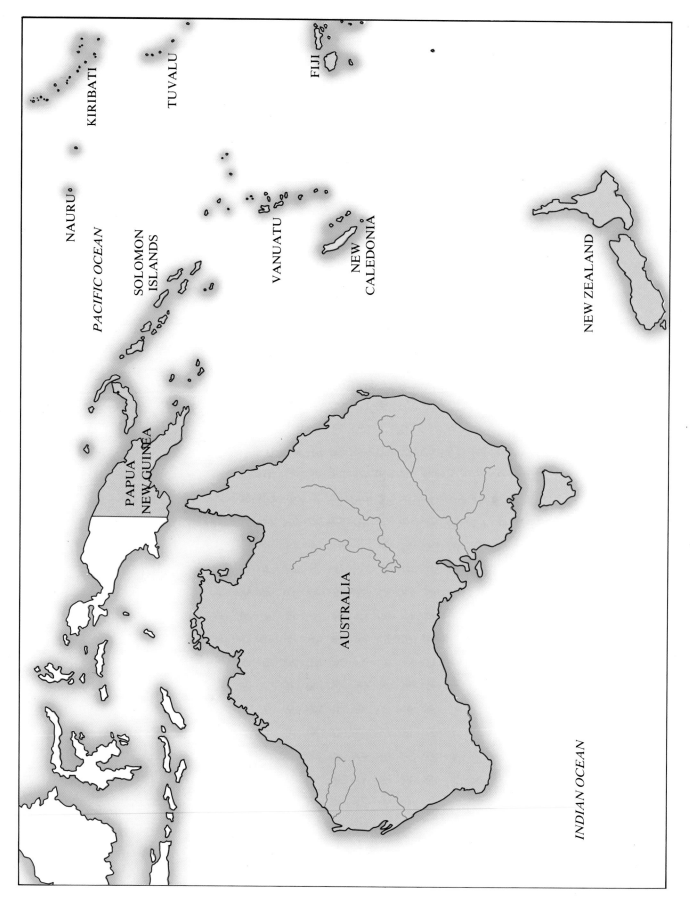

KIRIBATI

TUVALU

FIJI

NAURU

PACIFIC OCEAN

SOLOMON
ISLANDS

VANUATU

NEW
CALEDONIA

NEW ZEALAND

PAPUA
NEW GUINEA

AUSTRALIA

INDIAN OCEAN